HISTORIC
STORMS
—— OF ——
CAPE COD

HISTORIC
STORMS
OF
CAPE COD

DON WILDING

THE
History
PRESS

Published by The History Press
Charleston, SC
www.historypress.com

Front cover: Alton Kenney's boat yard in Chatham after the Hurricane of 1944. *Chapman Family Loggia Photo Collection.*

First published 2024

Manufactured in the United States

ISBN 9781467157261

Library of Congress Control Number: 2024931459

In loving memory of

John V. Wilding
December 18, 1929–April 1, 2006

CONTENTS

ACKNOWLEDGEMENTS

This book would not be possible without the help of a wide variety of friends, on and off Cape Cod:

Bill Burke at Cape Cod National Seashore; Rebekah Ambrose-Dalton at the William Brewster Nickerson Cape Cod History Archives of the Wilkens Library at Cape Cod Community College; Deb Rich at the Sandwich Town Archives, Sandwich Public Library; Glenn Field at the National Weather Service's Boston office; Barbara Amidon at the Lighthouse Inn in West Dennis; Linda Ersoy at the Sandcastle Resort in Provincetown; Dr. Graham Giese; Jack Clarke; Mildred Champlin; Eileen Seaboldt, Marca Daley and Patti Donohoe at the Eastham Historical Society; Michael Lach and the Harwich Conservation Trust; Henry Lind and the Eastham Conservation Foundation; Bob Dwyer, Kate Roderick, Teresa Izzo and everyone at the Cape Cod Museum of Natural History; Bob Seay, Shirley Weber, Debbie Abbott, Deborah Ullman, Laura Roskos and everyone at the Nauset Fellowship (UU), Chapel in the Pines, Eastham; Glenn and Sheila Mott; Joanne Twombley; Robby "The Dune Tramp" McQueeney; and Jon March.

I'm eternally grateful to Carol Dumas and Donna Tunney at the *Cape Codder* newspaper in Orleans, where some of the material in this book saw its first printed form in my "Shore Lore" columns, which ran between 2015 and 2021. Also, many thanks for the virtual visuals and tidbits of information from Ben Kettlewell, Lisa King and Salvador Vasques.

I'd also like to extend thanks to the dozens of organizations on Cape Cod and across New England that have hosted my Cape Cod history lectures since 2001.

There are many good people who are no longer with us who contributed to this effort in one way, shape or form over the years, more than they would ever know: Nan Turner Waldron, George and Rosemary Abbott, George Rongner, Phil Ryder, Noel Beyle, Jim Owens, Terri Rae Smith, Jared Collins and Harriet Wilding.

Finally, I could never have accomplished any of this without the love and support of my son, Matt Wilding; and my wife, Nita Wilding. Much love to you both.

—Don Wilding
Franklin, Massachusetts
November 2023

INTRODUCTION

*Every one of us needs to feel beyond self: to feel small
measured against distant horizons; to feel powerless against the winds;
to feel voiceless against the thunder of the storm.*
—*Nan Turner Waldron,* Journey to Outermost House

Out on Cape Cod, the weather can often be a highlight of any given season. Whenever a high-powered storm is charging up the coast, my phone begins to endlessly sound alerts: warnings, advisories…and a text from my longtime friend Jon March of Connecticut.

"It's blowing up," the words on the screen read. "I think we are going to have a northeaster."

Jon is quoting from the "Midwinter" chapter of Henry Beston's book *The Outermost House*, in which Bill Eldredge, a surfman from the Nauset Coast Guard Station in Eastham, is alerting the author to an approaching storm. It's become inside humor to us, since, like me, Jon is both a weather and *Outermost House* enthusiast. We've ventured out to the Cape's outer beach during several gales, most notably the blizzard of January 2005 and the Patriots Day storm of April 2007. Between us, Beston quotes fly about as frequently as sand grains in the storm-force winds.

As Amos Bronson Alcott wrote back in 1868, "The eye craves the spectacle of the horizon; [the spirit] actual contact with the elements, sympathy with the seasons as they rise and roll." I've identified with this mindset since my boyhood days during the 1960s, especially when it came to the stormy

A boy watches the high surf generated by Tropical Storm José at Coast Guard Beach in Eastham. José meandered off the coast for several days in September 2017. *Author's collection.*

extremes offered by Mother Nature. I was captivated by snowstorms in the winter and thunderstorms in the summer.

Weather reports were consumed more frequently than meals, whether it was in print or on the airwaves of radio and television. My father introduced me to KWO-35, the New York City area's National Weather Service radio outlet ("broadcasting on 162.55 megahertz"), which offered updated forecasts every six hours. I didn't miss too many of them; in fact, I used my dad's weather radio so much that he ended up giving it to me. In high school, one of my classmates, Robert Czaplicki ("Dr. Bob," I called him, as a complimentary nod to WOR-AM radio meteorologist Dr. Bob Harris), shared this enthusiasm. In fact, he predicted the impact of the Blizzard of '78 on the New York area a week before it buried northern New Jersey with a foot and a half of snow.

Some suggested that I pursue meteorology as a career. (I didn't.) Some have since suggested that I should have, and the need to follow what the elements were up to never left me. This is my fifth book, and all of them prominently feature great storms of Cape Cod.

In this book, heavy emphasis is put on the historic weather events, the benchmark storms, which always trigger the inquiry of "Where were you during the [insert storm name or date here]?" The hurricanes of 1938 and 1944, Carol and Edna in 1954, the Blizzard of '78, the 1987 northeaster that breached Chatham Bar, Hurricane Bob and the "No-Name Storm" (later christened the "Perfect Storm")—their stories and impact on the Cape are here. There's also a lengthy list of some of the "Notables and Near-Misses" of the twentieth and twenty-first centuries.

When I was a preschooler visiting the Pocono Mountains in Pennsylvania during the 1960s, a powerful thunderstorm raged one night. We visited a nearby stream and lake the following morning and saw all kinds of flood and wind damage, with erosion and downed trees. I asked my parents about it. "The storm did that," they said. "How?" I thought. I wanted to know more.

Since then, some of those questions have been answered, but the power exhibited by severe weather never fails to leave me amazed. As Nan Turner Waldron, who I often referred to as my "*Outermost* guru," wrote, "The thunder of a storm is one of the voices from the depths of the earth."

STORMS

A CAPE COD WAY OF LIFE

With the turn of the tide came fury unbelievable. The great rhythm of its waters now at one with the rhythm of the wind, the ocean rose out of the night to attack the ancient rivalry of earth, hurling breaker after thundering breaker against the long bulwark of sands.
—*Henry Beston,* The Outermost House, *1928*

For thousands of years, Cape Cod has been battered by the frequent northeasters and occasional hurricanes that unleash their elemental fury on this "bare and bended arm of Massachusetts," as Henry David Thoreau once called it.

Former Cape Cod National Seashore ranger Jack Clarke noted in a 2023 correspondence, "American history is marked by wars and presidencies. In coastal Massachusetts, we mark time with major storms—the Great New England Hurricane of 1938, the Blizzard of '78, the Perfect Storm."

Prior to the early days of the twentieth century, the toll of these tempests was often measured in terms of human lives, as opposed to material and natural destruction associated with more recent storms. Cyclones such as the Colonial Hurricane of 1635 and the *Portland* Gale of 1898 may be better known for their death tolls. After the loss of over six hundred New England lives in the Hurricane of 1938, preparation and awareness became priorities. In turn, with coastal building increasing, so did property damage during severe weather events, mostly northeasters and hurricanes.

High waves crash on the front porch of the Loggia beach camp in Chatham during a driving rainstorm on March 26, 1932. *Chapman family Loggia photo collection.*

Russell A. Lovell, historian of the town of Sandwich, was editor of the Sandwich Historical Society's newsletter, *The Acorn*, in 1973. He published an account of the Cape's stormy history in that periodical, which was reprinted in the *Cape Cod Independent* in January 1978:

> *Cape Cod has some special features which affect the damage storms can do here. Sustained high winds can push seawater far above high tide levels, especially in enclosed bays. Buzzards Bay collects high water in hurricane winds from the south. Cape Cod Bay fills up in northeasters. The shallows east and south of the Cape get very choppy in storms, just as the North Sea does.*

Every winter, Cape Codders brace for the dreaded northeasters. The peninsula is right in the path of these powerful low-pressure systems, which develop in the latitudes between Georgia and New Jersey, within one hundred miles east or west of the East Coast, according to the National Weather Service. These storms progress generally northeastward and typically attain maximum intensity near New England and the Maritime Provinces of Canada. The infamous Blizzard of 1978 and the *Portland* Gale are usually considered the benchmarks for this type of storm. The cost of damage from the worst storms can run into the billions of dollars.

In this undated photograph, an Eastham cottage on Coast Guard Beach was pushed off its foundation by a storm but found a second life on nearby Ocean View Drive. *Cape Cod National Seashore.*

Longtime meteorologist Don Kent noted the difference between the northeaster and the hurricane for *Cape Cod Life* in 1987:

> *A summer or early fall hurricane can pack an even stronger punch than northeaster, but it lasts only for a very short time, rather than the twenty-four hours or longer of a winter northeaster. The hurricane's severest damage may only be in a path forty miles wide, while the northeaster's peak strength is spread out over a much larger area.*

Hurricanes aren't frequent visitors to New England, but when they do come calling, they are often in clusters. Four significant hurricanes struck the Cape between 1938 and 1954, with two of them arriving within twelve days of each other. The name *hurricane* comes from the Mayan god Huracan, who, according to the account by the Chatham Historical Society's Josephine Buck Ivanoff in the *Cape Cod Chronicle*, "sent his thunderbolts and ferocious wind storms upon the people and blew the seas into raging fury that swept all creatures before him into death and destruction." Cape mariners would later "come face to face with Huracan's towering anger and developed a healthy respect for it."

Hurricanes are often caught up in the Gulf Stream on their way to New England. By the time these cyclones hit the colder waters off Cape Cod,

Above and opposite: An unidentified and undated pamphlet details some of the hazards of hurricanes on Cape Cod. *Sandwich Town Archives.*

they often take on what are called "extratropical" features. These storms usually originate either near the Cape Verde Islands off the African coast or in the Bahamas, according to Glenn Field, the warning coordination meteorologist of the Boston-area office of the National Weather Service in Norton, Massachusetts. Field described the differences in a 2023 interview:

> *The Cape Verde systems tend to be giant storms. They take over a week to cross the Atlantic. The Bahama storms tend to be smaller. They accelerate up the coast, but they give very little lead time. A rule of thumb—a storm has to be at 72 degrees West longitude to have a chance of hitting us. The point when New England needs to take action is when there's a named storm in the Bahamas. If it's off the North Carolina coast, you're late. You're already having impacts from the storm.*

This photograph by Danny Clarke shows some of the thousands of people who flocked to Eastham's Coast Guard Beach during the storm known as the Blizzard of '78 on February 7, 1978. *Cape Cod National Seashore.*

Field also listed "three rules of thumb" for New England hurricanes:

- *Forget about when the hurricane is going to make landfall. That's going to mislead everybody, because everything jumps ahead of the storm;*
- *You need to know where you are with respect to the track of the eye;*
- *If you want to figure out what the highest gust is at your house, if you're east of the track, you take the maximum sustained winds plus the forward motion of the storm. If you're west of the track, you can subtract the forward motion.*

A worst-case scenario, said Field, is a storm with the potency of the 1938 hurricane moving over New England again:

It's not a question of if, it's a question of when it will happen. In this case, a northern movement of the storm making landfall near Foxwoods in Connecticut, would have a twenty-foot surge in Narragansett Bay. If you bring the storm up Narragansett Bay, the water has nowhere to go in Buzzards Bay. There would be thirty feet at Parkwood Beach in Wareham. Hurricane Katrina's maximum storm surge was twenty-five feet.

On the Cape, many flock to the beaches to witness nature's power during a northeaster or hurricane. In 1990, John LoDico of the *Cape Codder* summed up Cape Codders' fascination with viewing hyped-up storms "as they would a good boxing match. The one-two combination of wind and water may have left some residents on the (financial) ropes, but it brought the spectators to their feet."

During the 1978 blizzard, thousands of cars lined the roads leading up to Coast Guard Beach in Eastham to watch the raging sea. "The traffic issues became pretty severe," Henry Lind, Eastham's longtime natural resources officer, recalled in a 2008 interview. Essayist Robert Finch was one of those who made it out to Coast Guard Beach, marveling at how the dunes and bathhouse were being destroyed by the incoming surf. Finch recalled the scene in a 2014 interview: "There were hundreds of people there, watching the waves smash up against the bathhouse. And with every wave, the crowds would just cheer. And I said, 'Why is that? What are we cheering about?' That stuck in my mind."

Following the No-Name Storm of 1991, LoDico noted that there were some residents who would not recover from the northeaster's devastation but then concluded:

> *For most, [it] was just another unpredictable occurrence, something to be reckoned with immediately with sandbags and hurricane lamps, then remembered, through photographs and old newspaper clippings and through stories that inevitably, and fortunately, will be handed down for years to come.*

THE GREAT NEW ENGLAND HURRICANE OF 1938

Then came the dawn. Words cannot describe it. To the writer, whose own newspaper plant had been under six feet of water, the thought came to him as it must have to all who sustained like losses, that the blow was too great to realize. Where to begin, what to do. Nobody knew but everybody began to do something, futile as it might seem.
—*Wareham newspaper editor Lemuel Hall, as reported by the* Harwich Independent, *October 6, 1938*

D uring the early afternoon hours of September 21, 1938, Alice Maurer and her nephew Henry Maurer ventured into Falmouth to run some errands. Rainy weather was in the offing, but the forty-one-year-old nurse, a longtime visitor to the Fells area of Falmouth, and her nephew stayed out a bit longer to do some shopping.

However, the weather conditions quickly deteriorated—so badly, in fact, that Alice Maurer and several other people would not return home that day. The deadliest hurricane in the history of New England was closing in fast.

Meteorologists have long told the story that there was so little warning of the Hurricane of 1938 that beachgoers were enjoying late-summer weather while the storm brewed offshore and was about to hit in a matter of hours. Most of the people in its path were completely unaware of what was heading their way.

As the Maurers headed for home, the car's gas gauge reading plummeted close to empty. Henry suggested that they stop and get the tank filled, but

The waterfront area of the Woods Hole section of Falmouth saw a storm surge of historic proportions during the Great New England Hurricane of 1938. *NOAA*.

his aunt, in a hurry to get home, felt they had sufficient fuel. Keep going, she said.

It would prove to be a fatal mistake.

Along Beach Road, the car ran out of gas near the Moors Pavilion. South of Beach Road, the high tide was rolling in from Vineyard Sound, but this wasn't just any high tide. This was a storm surge of historic proportions.

As the Maurers sat in their car, E. Gunnar Peterson arrived at the scene. He took Henry to get gas and, according to the *Falmouth Enterprise*, "urged Miss Maurer to come as well, but she preferred to stay in the car and watch the surf."

When Peterson and Henry Maurer returned to the scene, the car was in the pond, and Alice was nowhere to be found. However, as the *Falmouth Enterprise* noted, a group of sightseers watching the surf were "unwilling witnesses" to Alice Maurer's demise. One of the witnesses, Eleanor Brooks, said that the waves broke over the top of the pavilion, eventually destroying it, and "across the shore road in flat, angry waves of muddy water." A car drove up, and Brooks sent the passengers back to the fire department for help. A figure was spotted through the ever-increasing water but faded into the storm. A boy tried to swim out for a rescue but couldn't make it and turned back. Alice Maurer's body was found shortly after the storm.

A Storm for the Ages

Known as the "Great New England Hurricane of 1938" and the "Long Island Express," the storm took shape off the Cape Verde Islands on September 4. Taking an unusual track over the Gulf Stream, the storm continued to intensify while tracking northward at nearly 60 miles per hour, making landfall on Long Island and again in Milford, Connecticut, on September 21. Winds were devastating, with the Blue Hill Observatory in Milton, Massachusetts, recording the strongest winds ever for the region. Sustained winds were measured at 121 miles per hour, and gusts reached 186 miles per hour. Roofs, trees and crops were extensively damaged, and power outages were widespread, lasting for weeks in some areas. Over 600 people were killed and another 1,700 injured in southern New England.

According to the National Weather Service, the eye of the storm made landfall at the time of astronomical high tide, still moving north at fifty-one miles per hour. Unlike most storms, this hurricane did not weaken on its way toward southern New England, due to its rapid forward speed and track. This unleashed a substantial storm surge in the region, causing eighteen- to twenty-five-foot tides from New London, Connecticut, east to Cape Cod. The downtown area of Providence, Rhode Island, was covered with twenty feet of ocean water. Sections of Falmouth and New Bedford were submerged under eight feet of water.

The ordinary tide in Buzzards Bay flooded over Wareham and the Buzzards Bay section of Bourne and made shambles out of Onset's Main Street. "It ripped down cottage after cottage at Gray Gables and Monument Beach," the *Hyannis Patriot* reported the day after the storm.

According to the *New Bedford Standard-Times*, residents of the Cape "began to abandon their homes for the safety of higher ground. Many remained too long, fighting to save their homes and belongings, and met death." Survivors told "of the roaring of the wind, the cracking of timber as their homes gave way, the relentless power of the waves that swept buildings about like match boxes."

Five residents of one of the Gray Gables cottages lost their lives when the structure dropped into Buzzards Bay and was swept into the Cape Cod Canal, finally coming to rest against the north side of the Bourne Bridge. The victims were removed from a hole in the cottage's roof.

Back in Falmouth, Andrew S. Jones and his wife of Silver Beach were also among the drowning victims. The couple had celebrated their golden anniversary just fourteen months earlier, but when the monster tides began

A cottage that was swept away by a storm surge from the Gray Gables area of Bourne is shown in the Cape Cod Canal at the north side of the Bourne Bridge. Five people perished inside the structure. *Sandwich Town Archives.*

to pour into their yard, they fled into their house and then up to the roof. The surging tides soon ripped the roof off the house and carried it away, with the Joneses still on board. The *Falmouth Enterprise* reported that two neighbors, who were at the Florence Tea Room, saw the couple's predicament and tried to tie blankets together to throw as lifelines, but the wind swept away their attempt. The roof raft finally crashed to bits against another house.

Converging tides from Buzzards Bay and Vineyard Sound combined to bring what resembled a tidal wave to Woods Hole, the *Enterprise* reported. Columbus O. Iselin II, an oceanographer at the Oceanographic Institution, told the *Enterprise* that he believed that it was congestion of the water that caused the Woods Hole flood: "I am convinced that the water rose here because it was caught in a bottle neck. It had no place else to go. The tide was rising just as the wind was rising."

William T. Briggs and Albert W. Neal of Woods Hole and John A. Steadman, Hayward Webster and Frederick Lilja of the patrol boat *General Greene* were among the drowning victims at the southernmost tip of Falmouth, the *Enterprise* reported.

Briggs had been the caretaker of the F.A. Park estate for the previous eight years. While checking on the Park boathouse near his residence, he waded through the swift and rising current of the floodwaters. After Briggs lost his

Converging tides from Buzzards Bay and Vineyard Sound combined to bring abnormally high tides to Woods Hole during the storm. *NOAA.*

Damage along Falmouth's waterfront was extensive due to the high tides generated by the hurricane. *Author's collection.*

balance and fell into the water, his son, Edward, tried to throw him a rope, but the tide swept away Briggs right before his son's eyes. Briggs's wife, who had recently undergone surgery, was rescued by men who waded through five feet of water.

Neal drowned while working at a Penzance Point estate. With the tide sweeping in from Great Harbor, both men grabbed a board protruding from the house, but another tidal surge swept the sixty-year-old Neal out to sea after two hours of struggling to stay afloat. Neal's son Milton was rescued by Wayne Senate after clinging to a pole for three and a half hours.

Penzance summer resident Albert Borden witnessed the drowning of Webster and Lilja, two Coast Guardsmen. After 5:00 p.m., Borden, the two victims and two other men were engaged in rescue work at Penzance, where they were carrying people from flooded houses. Borden told the *Enterprise*:

> *As we neared the Frank J. Frost house, the rushing tide that had crossed from the harbor to the bay came roaring back. We tried to run through the water across the broken road but any speed was impossible. Suddenly what appeared to be a solid wall of water tore out of Buzzards Bay and picked us up as it rolled toward the Hole. Before I knew it I was abreast of the George Clowes yacht about 30 yards from shore. I grabbed the anchor chain and was hauled on deck by members of the crew.*

Borden said that Ned Harvey, swept over to the Bureau of Fisheries dock, managed to hold on to the pilings and made it to shore. Steadman, the radio operator, was also swept away. "We were the last to see the two coast guard fellows," Borden said. "All I can remember is hearing one of them shout that he couldn't swim."

Millfield Street in Falmouth was "a torrent of rushing water." James McInnis and Ware Cattell, in a rowboat, stopped by several houses to retrieve people and bring them to safety. After dark, they were the ones who had to be rescued. Amy Billings and her daughter Edith were flooded out of their home and had to wait for rescue perched on the crossbeam of the clothesline support in the yard until the rescue boat arrived. At Nobska Beach, twenty-foot waves broke over the road, carrying the Fay bathhouse across the swamp pond. Viewed from the hill on the Woods Hole side, "Nobska Light looked a beacon on an island," the *Enterprise* noted. The summer house of J. Edward Gallagher, once located near Falmouth Heights, was seen floating in the harbor. On the bluffs in front of the Terrace Gables Hotel in Falmouth Heights, a cave-in carried away part of the street.

This page: Storm tides tore many structures apart along the shorelines of Falmouth. *Author's collection.*

The train station in the Buzzards Bay section of Bourne was flooded by several feet of water from the Cape Cod Canal. The canal's train bridge is in the background. *Sandwich Town Archives.*

The paper also reported this item from the downtown area:

At the First Methodist Church, a loud cracking sounding like the mere ripping of linen could be heard, as the steeple was swaying and slipping. Patrolman Eckhardt H. Sparre had the front of the church roped off just before the steeple came crashing down. Fortunately, no one was hit by debris.

Buzzards Bay and Wareham also saw their share of fatalities. According to the *Hyannis Patriot*, one woman drowned in the Main Street area of Buzzards Bay, while two others drowned at the Taylor estate, near the Cape Cod Canal entrance. Another man drowned at Onset. Five people drowned in Wareham.

In Wareham, a *Brockton Enterprise* photographer took a picture of a house turned on its side. It was one of many that "were swept far from their original locations." The *Taunton Daily Gazette* reported that "houses at crazy angles were found by their owners and steps were almost immediately taken to either right them or tear them down." A Hamilton Beach house was swept

Train tracks in the Buzzards Bay section of Bourne were heavily damaged by the storm tides from the Cape Cod Canal. *Sandwich Town Archives.*

Hundreds of trees were uprooted along the roads in Sandwich. *Sandwich Town Archives.*

two miles before it landed near the railroad bridge. Whatever trees didn't blow down were badly damaged when wreckage drifted against them at Swifts Beach.

Main Street in Buzzards Bay, under three feet of water, was closed from 6:30 p.m. to midnight. Every store building, the theater and the fire station were flooded. Two oil tanks were knocked over, spilling fuel all over the highway. The train station, located just off the canal, was also flooded.

In Onset, the tide tossed two fifty-foot schooners in the highway to the approach of the Point Independence Bridge. The tide "distributed bits of the Kenney Taffy Shop at the pier, all over the highway, and mixed the pieces with fishing vessels," the *Patriot* reported. Railroad damage was also substantial—the Cohasset Narrows Bridge and several hundred feet of track south were undermined and made impassable. Several hundred feet of track in Pocasset was damaged. In Sandwich, hundreds of trees were uprooted along the main roads.

LESS EXTREME TO THE EAST

"Serious as was the situation in Bourne and Falmouth, we believe that the rest of the Cape was indeed fortunate," the *Harwich Independent* reported in its September 29, 1938 edition. "The Lower Cape escaped with less damage, although winds were high," the *Cape Cod Standard-Times* added. In her book *Dennis, Cape Cod: From Firstcomers to Newcomers, 1639–1993*, Nancy Thacher Reid wrote for the Dennis Historical Society:

> *The town was spared expensive damage, aside from downed wires and a few lost trees. It was fortunate that the track of the storm was to our west, and that no storm surge occurred. A large problem, which had to be solved, was the disposal of fallen limbs and trees. Special brush dumps were established to prevent an overload at the town dump.*

In Harwich, "one of the most heroic of hurricane rescues on Cape Cod" occurred, according to newspaper reports from an unidentified article in a scrapbook in the Nickerson Archives of Cape Cod Community College. Charles Bevins of Harwich Port carried Mrs. George Kissick to safety from her flooded home at South Harwich Beach. Kissick called Harwich Police when the water reached a level of three feet on the first floor, and Patrolman

Lawrence Homer attempted to reach the residence, but his car was almost rolled over by the surf. Bevins, who followed police to the beach, waded into the surf and swam part of the way to the marooned house after having been several times thrown back by the surf. He found Kissick standing on a table, just out of reach of the rising water.

Boats were piled up on the bank of Wychmere Harbor after the highest tide there in fifty years. A forty-eight-foot yawl dragged its mooring and was lifted out of the water to rest wrecked on Reuben Kendrick's wharf. Cat boats, knockabouts and small boats piled together elsewhere.

Along Nauset Beach in Orleans, several beach camps were washed away, Frances L. Higgins noted in her book *Drifting Memories: The Nauset Beach Camps on Cape Cod*.

Provincetown was spared the wrath unleashed on the Upper Cape region, as the tide began to recede as the storm hit. The *Provincetown Advocate* reported that the wind hurled tons of sand from the shore against buildings on Commercial Street: "In the vicinity of Howland Street, the main street looked more like the beach."

The report "A New England Hurricane: A Factual, Pictorial Record" noted:

> As the sky darkened in Provincetown and the wind became an eerie screaming whistle, fishermen uttered strange prophecies. "Wait'll high tide. High tide's due at 10 o'clock. Goodbye Provincetown." Fortunately, the storm had spent itself before high tide came in. Gardens were destroyed and a few small fishing craft succumbed, but on the whole, the town's fleet rode out the gale gallantly.

In her book *Time and the Town*, Mary Heaton Vorse had this to say about the storm: "While the hurricane of 1938 was less severe for Provincetown than the Gale [of 1898], had there been high tide and slight change of wind when the hurricane struck, the town might have been washed from its moorings."

The storm was not without peril, however. A ninety-foot schooner broke loose from its moorings and went on a dangerous ride through the harbor before being brought under control by the Coast Guard. Fred Salvadore's dragger *Stella* was driven ashore on the bulkhead and wharf at Commander Donald MacMillan's home, according to the *Cape Cod Standard-Times*.

Reports: Cape Cod Swept Away

At the storm's height, Cape Cod was cut off from the rest of the state. Only the Radio Marine station in Chatham served as a communications base. "The result was the circulation of wild rumors about the Cape being entirely underwater, Provincetown being destroyed, and other fantastic tales," the *Yarmouth Register* reported.

According to the *Provincetown Advocate*, "Every person who has reached Provincetown since the storm has been halted often by police and National Guardsmen, and informed that he couldn't get to Provincetown because it had been wiped off the map!" was the telephone message that William F. Gilman of the Town Criers Association had for WBZ radio in Boston on September 28. Those erroneous reports made their way through the media. Gilman phoned in to WBZ to set the record straight:

> *For the sake of the feelings of people whose relatives and friends live on the Lower Cape, please broadcast the accurate facts concerning Cape Cod's post-hurricane situation. I think this story should be refuted once and for all. The only way it can be done is to give the real facts as much prominence as given to the original false reports. The Town Criers Association is appreciative of efforts by a few newspapers to correct the confusion.*

One Provincetown woman was traveling on a bus from New Bedford, according to Mary Heaton Vorse's book *Time and the Town*. The bus had to turn around at the bridge to Fairhaven after a schooner, carried by a wave, hit the bridge. The woman went to a New Bedford hotel, but as she arrived, she "heard the loudspeaker announce that the Cape didn't exist, that it had been swept away, that nothing had been heard from it for hours."

After the storm, messengers arrived by truck and carted away more than four hundred telegrams to be cleared through Boston. What was the general drift of the telegrams? "Well after reading and hearing erroneous Cape news bulletins, people were scribbling, 'I'm OK. Are you? Answer at once,'" the *Advocate* reported.

Fortunately for all involved, word got out that Provincetown and the rest of the Outer Cape were still indeed above sea level, according to the *Advocate*: "For a time it seemed as though it might take its pick of the town with it. But the tip of the Cape, itself created by the fury of wind and sea, took it square on the chin, shuddered, rocked a bit and stood firm."

In an editorial, the *Falmouth Enterprise* said that "the Cape Cod Canal being choked with debris probably gets the plum for tall stories, although the Hearst newspaper with the headline '77 dead on Cape' finishes well to the front." The *Harwich Independent* also scolded the off-Cape newspapers for unprofessional behavior:

> *For the daily newspapers to broadcast the erroneous impression that we were washed off the map, blown into the Atlantic and our shore line completely altered, was adding far more injury to the Cape than the damage sustained by Falmouth and Bourne. To the credit of the Cape Cod daily, they gave emphatic denial to these false news reports and helped materially to correctly inform the public so unnecessarily alarmed by Boston headlines.*

The *Hyannis Patriot* reported the story of how the obituary of Mrs. Thomas Beaupre of Buzzards Bay, and formerly of Hyannis, was published in Hyannis, Boston and New York newspapers. An unidentified woman, thought to be Beaupre, had washed ashore, but Beaupre and her husband had gone to Brockton just before the storm hit. "She walked into the Bourne Police Station and reported herself very much alive, much to the relief of friends and relatives. The story goes that she asked whether someone was looking for her. 'Yes, the undertaker,' replied one of the policemen."

Lighter Moments in the Mayhem

While the storm left more than its share of destruction in its wake, there were some lighter moments as well, published in the *Falmouth Enterprise*:

- An inebriated Bourne man went to bed just as the storm began and slept through it all. Upon waking the next morning, he found the steps of his house gone and the water within three inches of the floor of his house;
- The paper printed a report of how, somewhere north of Old Silver Beach in Falmouth, the storm left a dory stranded in the top of a pine tree;
- Reports of looting were common on the Upper Cape after the storm. Among the reported stolen items—a three-hundred-

gallon water tank at the bathhouses at Silver Beach. "Nothing seems to be safe anymore," the paper said;

- A couple was taken from their Menauhant home by rowboat. They tried to save the dinner cooking in the kitchen when they were alerted they needed to evacuate and were taken across the street to a neighbor's home. Two maids who had been cooking the dinner packed the hot roast beef and fresh spinach in the rowboat. The meal was spilled into the water, but the roast beef was recovered. "The beef, in spite of its salt water bath, was served and enjoyed later," the paper reported;

- An up-Cape train ended up being stranded between Buzzards Bay and Wareham, thanks to the storm damage on the tracks and bridges. A reporter came by at 2:00 a.m., noticing that the train seemed ready to go but no one was on board. He asked one of the train men about the situation. The reply: "Well buddy, we've got a nice train here, and about a mile of track to play with. What do you think we ought to do?"

More to Come

During the summer of 1938, the former Bass River Lighthouse was sold by Harry E. Noyes to Massachusetts state senator Everett Stone for $21,000, with $1,000 contributions from three family members, including his twenty-year-old son, Robert. The West Dennis property would soon become known as the Lighthouse Inn and was still a thriving business in 2023. In a history compiled by the Lighthouse Inn's owners, Robert Stone told the story of hitching a ride from Boston to the Cape to see how much damage had been done to the property. It would not be the last time Stone and the Lighthouse Inn would have to face the wrath of a hurricane.

THE GREAT ATLANTIC HURRICANE OF 1944

Keeper [Octave] *Ponsart, said, "They are gone to the bottom. The iron ship. The iron men. They are all gone." Seamond cried, "All my uncles? All the sailors?" Her father wept openly, "Yes, Seamond, they are all gone."*
—*Captain W. Russell Webster, U.S. Coast Guard,*
on the loss of the Vineyard *lightship in 1944,* Naval History Magazine, *U.S. Naval Institute, February 2000*

On the night of September 14, 1944, *Vineyard* lightship No. 73, at its usual station near Cuttyhunk Island at the mouth of Vineyard Sound, went to the bottom during the raging Great Atlantic Hurricane. Twelve men perished.

Harold Flagg of Sandwich was among the seventeen crew members of the *Vineyard*, yet he and four other crew members were among the survivors. They were on leave in New Bedford and were unable to return to their posts due to the high seas and winds.

In June 2003, Flagg recalled his experiences for a meeting of the nonprofit group Tales of Cape Cod in Barnstable, as reported by Brad Lynch of the *Barnstable Patriot*: "The experience has been bugging me for 59 years. I think of them, every day. And I get teary every time I think of them."

Unlike the Great New England Hurricane of 1938, Cape Cod and the Northeast were more prepared for the onslaught of the 1944 cyclone. First identified east of the Lesser Antilles on September 4, the disturbance gradually intensified by September 9 and curved northward. By September 13, it was a

Twelve lives were lost when the *Vineyard* lightship was overcome by the stormy seas on September 14, 1944. *National Archives.*

Category 5 hurricane north of the Bahamas before making landfall on Long Island and the Rhode Island coast as a Category 2 storm on September 14. On Cape Cod, the storm caused over $5 million in damage, mostly due to lost boats, fallen trees and utility damage.

The center of the storm passed over Providence, Rhode Island, and then the Blue Hill area in Milton, Massachusetts. The Cape was on the east side of the storm, just far enough away from the eye, resulting in the high winds. However, the height of the winds did not coincide with high tide. The lowest barometer readings were taken at Squaw Island, Hyannisport, at 28.85 inches, and 28.78 inches in Falmouth.

Thirty-one people perished in the Northeast, but no lives were lost on the Cape. On September 18, 1983, the *Village Advertiser* newspaper recalled the tropical system's arrival: "The storm reached its height in the early morning hours, with rain and high winds permanently altering the face of Cape Cod and the Islands. Fortunately, high tide had passed nearly three hours before the storm peaked, a stroke of luck that people in 1938 did not share."

However, luck was not on the side of the *Vineyard* lightship crew or anyone else at sea. The hurricane sank five ships, claiming 344 lives at sea. Under orders to remain at its station, the crew of the *Vineyard* was forced to ride out the storm. During the early morning hours of September 15, as the region was being battered by winds of 105 miles per hour and a storm surge of eight to ten feet, bright lights were spotted in the vicinity of the lightship's location. "Six red and white distress flares coming from the area of the *Vineyard* just after midnight," wrote Captain W. Russell Webster of the U.S. Coast Guard for the Naval History Institute's *Naval History Magazine*. When the storm abated, the lightship was gone.

The Ponsart family, who lived at the Cuttyhunk Island Lighthouse, was hit particularly hard by the loss of the *Vineyard*'s crew, particularly the keeper, Octave, and his five-year-old daughter, Seamond. Coast Guardsmen from the nearby lightships often stayed with the Ponsarts and had developed a special bond with them. Seamond often referred to these men as her "uncles." During the storm, the Ponsarts struggled to keep the lighthouse lamp burning, as the waves and winds frequently doused it. According to a report for the Commonwealth of Massachusetts, the Board of Underwater Archaeological Resources noted, "Coast Guard officials reported only that the lightship was 'off station.' As it was wartime and the government feared public hysteria, a media blackout was in effect until the exact cause of the vessel's sinking could be determined." The report also said that on September 23, navy divers found the sunken vessel:

> *Although its masts and funnel were snapped off at the deck, the mooring chains were still secure, indicating the lightship foundered while on station.*
>
> *It was theorized that the doors used to load coal through the hull had collapsed under pounding seas, flooding the ship. However, when sport divers first located the hull nineteen years later, this theory could not be substantiated. It was discovered that the hull plates in the area near where the storm anchor once hung were stove in. Normally, the three to five ton mushroom anchor was deployed in heavy weather. If the crew was unable to drop this anchor, it is likely that high seas would have slammed it against the hull.*

Lost in the tragedy were Captain Edgar Sevigny, Vangel Constantine, Joseph George Gordon, Jack M. Hammett, Allen Leslie Hull, John Kolozsky, Peter Paul Michalak, Lawrence Roland Starratt, Edward Walter Steckling, Frederick Julius Stellten, John Joseph Stimac and Richard Talbot. According to a 2003 article in *Martha's Vineyard Magazine*, Stimac was Flagg's roommate and had only joined the *Vineyard* crew a few weeks earlier.

According to Captain W. Russell Webster, Flagg and the other four survivors learned of the tragic news upon their arrival at Cuttyhunk on September 15. A team of seven divers returned to the site of the tragedy, about a mile from its station, and recovered the lightship's bell. The bell made stops at the Cape Cod National Seashore and on board the *New Bedford* lightship, but after the vessel fell into a state of disrepair, Flagg began a campaign to save the bell. A deal was later struck to license the bell to the City of New Bedford. The bell's new location on the New Bedford waterfront was dedicated in September 1999.

"We vowed, the five of us, that as long as one of us stays alive, these men and this ship will be remembered," Flagg said at his Tales of Cape Cod talk in 2003.

DEVASTATION IN DENNIS

As is the case with many hurricanes on Cape Cod, the shoreline along Nantucket Sound sustained the most damage during the storm. One of the headlines in the *Cape Cod Standard-Times* read: "Central Lower areas hit harder than Canal and Falmouth sections."

The town of Dennis was among the most devastated areas, as the Lower County Road, Route 28 and Upper County Road bridges were destroyed and hundreds of trees were taken down. The *Yarmouth Register* reported that Lower County Road was under eight feet of water. Electricity was out for over three weeks, and schools remained closed for the rest of September.

Phyllis Horton, who was sixteen at the time of the storm, told this story that was published in the *Yarmouth Register*: "My father had to swim part way home to Dennisport from the fire station on Old Main Street to let the cows out of the barn. They swam away, and Saturday morning he rounded them up in West Harwich. Our bull drowned in the meadow."

"The village of West Dennis was hit with the most devastating blow in its history," the *Yarmouth Register* reported. Trees that surrounded the Toy Village cottage colony were leveled. The steeple of the West Dennis Methodist Church was torn off and "driven like a spear into the church roof."

The *Yarmouth Register* told the ordeal of Mr. and Mrs. Bertram Smith, year-round residents and storm survivors at West Dennis Beach since 1917. The Smiths saw their house torn to pieces within ten minutes, leaving them in waist-deep water and nothing but the clothes they were wearing. Their garage and car were destroyed, and his grocery truck was thrown on its side. The *Yarmouth Register* reported that twenty-seven cottages east of the Lighthouse Inn on West Dennis Beach were completely demolished.

Several cottages at the Lighthouse Inn in West Dennis were pushed inland by the storm surge. *Lighthouse Inn, West Dennis, Massachusetts.*

The Lighthouse Inn, which had seen its business grow since the Stone family purchased it in 1938, took a beating. In June, a new dining room and kitchen were constructed, but they didn't survive the storm. The inn compiled a historic dateline of its business, which further detailed what happened during the storm:

> *The brand new three month-old dining room was completely wiped out and left in sticks at the bridge where the Sand Bar is now. The Guest House and the oceanfront cottages were wiped off their foundations and pushed toward the back of the property. Cottage 16 was pushed as far back as the current Carriage House locations. Sand and debris covered the entire property. The Lodge had been pushed off its foundation and when put back, was raised by three cinder blocks in anticipation of future floods. There had been a small "L" off the back of the Lodge and this portion of the building was torn off and found resting out by Lighthouse Road and the small bridge. This small "L" would eventually be moved and made into Cottage 17. The entire foundation and support on the water side of the Main House had been washed away. Everett Stone, his son, Robert, and their crew had to quickly shore up the foundation with piers or the whole first floor over the sunroom and porch would have caved in.*

Opposite, top: The Lighthouse Inn's new dining room area, built only three months earlier, was completely wiped out by flooding from the 1944 storm. *Lighthouse Inn, West Dennis, Massachusetts.*

Opposite, bottom: The Lighthouse Inn's new dining room area, shortly after its construction in the spring of 1944. *Lighthouse Inn, West Dennis, Massachusetts.*

Above: The Lighthouse Inn has a ship model on display over a fireplace. Following the 1944 storm, a boy took the model from the damaged inn, but it was recovered by Bob Stone. *Lighthouse Inn, West Dennis, Massachusetts.*

As the storm was winding down, Bob Stone witnessed a boy "walking on the street with a ship model wrapped in one of the inn's bedspreads. The model had been over the fireplace in the new dining room, and one line was broken on it." Stone retrieved the ship model from the young lad, and as of 2023, it was still displayed at the inn.

The Stones spent the entire fall, winter and spring seasons repairing the damage. A new dining room was built on the first floor with an extended lobby; damage was repaired with some of the lumber from the dining room. The first dining room and kitchen were built on the second floor with steel girders as their basis. As the exhibit notes, "There were other hurricanes to hit Cape Cod in the following years but none wreaked as much damage on the Inn as the Great Atlantic Hurricane of 1944."

CARNAGE CAPE-WIDE

Just to the west of Dennis, across Bass River, the town of Yarmouth was experiencing similar issues after the storm. The *Yarmouth Register* reported that Stanley Eldridge of Yarmouth Port recorded a barometer reading of 28.98 at 1:00 a.m. the night of the storm. Frank Syme reported the same reading at 11:00 p.m. before having to evacuate his home: "Mr. Syme reported that the needle vibrated, a very unusual occurrence."

South Yarmouth and Bass River sustained heavy losses, especially with trees. The transmission tower for the radio station WOCB was split in two. The causeway to Great Island was so badly washed away that residents had to travel back and forth to the mainland in a bulldozer or by boat to Hyannis. On Berry Avenue, the entrance to Englewood Beach, the tide extended back about a quarter of a mile, carrying heavy wreckage with it.

The *Cape Cod Standard-Times* reported that the Parker's River Bridge on Route 28 in West Yarmouth was washed out, and the country restaurant Libby's Chowder House was moved from its foundations. The surging surf picked up the Chowder House oyster bar and placed it right in the middle of Route 28. River waters carried away the restaurant's equipment and furnishings. The *Yarmouth Register* told the story of a black-and-white pig that wandered out on the road at the Parker's River Bridge the morning after the storm: "He went from one to another of a group of people who were standing there looking at the wreckage, looking for some kind person to take care of him. After a while, disappointed in his search, he went off into the woods again."

The *Harwich Independent* reported that in Harwich, Lieutenant Lynden Wardell of Second Company State Guard had his men drive through the storm and evacuate seventy-nine women and children and eighteen men. They removed them to the Armory in West Dennis, where they remained all night without cots. A private attempted to make one more trip but barely escaped with his life, as his car was totally destroyed after it was carried off the highway near Swan River.

Every home along the beach from Sea Street to Wyndemere Bluffs suffered extensive damage; washing machines and refrigerators were carried hundreds of feet from their original positions. The McKissock house in South Harwich was gone, and the Hickey residence on Pilgrim Road was wrecked. At Wychmere Harbor in Harwich Port, smaller craft were crushed, and a seventeen-ton Coast Guard boat landed high and dry on the bank near the main road.

The *Independent* also noted, "One of the freaks of the storm was the odor of dill pickles, which filled the air for several day as the brine from the ocean was driven several miles from the water."

The *Barnstable Patriot* told of the ordeal of the Jennings family in Osterville, whose Dowse's Point cottage drifted for a half mile. Frances Jennings of Boston and Maryland was visiting her elderly father, William John Jennings, for ten days at his cottage, which extends into East Bay. At 10:50 p.m., they lost power, followed by storm surge water coming in under the door. Frances then heard her father call her frantically to come and help him hold the outside door of the living room shut. She retrieved two life jackets out of the garage and tied both of them on, and then both of them went into the sailboat in the garage, taking their flashlight, suitcases and valuables.

Just as they left the room, the door and windows caved in with a rush of water, which reached waist deep. She called to her neighbor Leland Eldridge to help. The whole structure then broke loose and floated into the bay. She managed to climb back into the house and grabbed on to the overturned boat, which came by them in the pitch darkness. Soon they felt bushes around their feet—the water was receding. They later learned that the tide had risen ten feet above the usual sea level.

The *Patriot* also reported on the plight of a Pittsburgh family summering at a cottage in Hyannis Port. They were rescued by a Coast Guard commander who circled each member of the family with a rope and then, proceeding in mountain-climbing fashion, led the party to safety. The family dog, which also had the line around him, slipped from his noose and swam safely to shore.

According to the *Yarmouth Register*, the office cottage of Congressman Charles L. Gifford was completely wrecked. His garage was undermined, and water covered it, destroying two cars. A piano and violin were ruined, and two thousand books were lost.

William White, the custodian of the Oyster Harbors riding stables on Little Island, risked his life to save six saddle horses during the height of the storm. White, shoulder deep in water, forced open the doors to the stalls and let the horses free to swim along with the rush of tide water to a point of safety on Oyster Harbor Island. To keep from drowning, White climbed to the top of the stable until the hurricane subsided.

In Hyannis, the Ocean Street bulkhead and Baxter Wharf section saw boats of all sizes tossed into backyards on Pleasant Street. A section of buildings adjoining the Hyannis Fish Company was completely swept away, and small buildings were washed from their foundations. Midshipmen from the Massachusetts Maritime Academy rescued a middle-aged woman, an eighteen-year old girl and seven other children from the second story of a home on Ocean Street, where the water rolled over the bulkhead. The midshipmen worked in neck-deep water against a rough surf.

Falmouth saw significant damage but not quite on the level of the 1938 storm. The *Boston Herald* reported that the ketch *Atlantis*, which came to the Woods Hole Oceanographic Institute from Holland in 1932, was swept ashore at Woods Hole. According to the *Falmouth Enterprise*, the main part of the Megansett Yacht Club was swept away and ended up as wreckage on the Cataumet shore. The *Yarmouth Register* reported that the J. Edward Gallagher house on the Heights side of the harbor, which was carried into the water during the 1938 storm, was swept off its foundation again and blown away.

The Woods Hole Steamboat Wharf was damaged by a fishing boat carrying seventy-five thousand pounds of fish that was trying to ride out the storm in the harbor. Wharf agent Robert Neal telephoned the New Haven offices in Boston every half hour until 11:45 p.m., when he gave his final report of the night: "The water is coming across the station floor and I'm getting the hell out." He got back to his house a half mile away to find a tree cracked at the base and having landed squarely on his kitchen. The wind caught it again and broke it back the other way. The only damage to the kitchen was a loosened blind and three loose shingles. No window glass or dishes in the kitchen were broken.

Red paint was flying around Little Harbor during the storm, the *Enterprise* reported. A paint storage shed for buoys at the Coast Guard headquarters was demolished by the wind. Some of the cans opened and distributed the paint. Grass at the headquarters was tinted red, and splotches decorated nearby trees. "Many of the unopened cans lost their labels and painters won't know if a can is battleship gray or buoy red until they open a can," the paper said.

The *Enterprise* also told the story of Harriet Baldwin fleeing her residence after downed electrical wires struck the house: "She was carrying a baby of 15 months. Two other children tagged along. The wire was sparking. The live wire whipped across Mrs. Baldwin's back and she was knocked unconscious (suffering third degree burns). The infant's clothing was scorched."

The *Enterprise* said that L.C. Small's greenhouses in North Falmouth were damaged, with many pines down around them. The paper also noted that his cow was unharmed: "Mr. Small's cow must have spent the night ducking trees."

This page: Extensive damage is shown at Alton Kenney's boat yard in Chatham. *Chapman family Loggia photo collection.*

The hurricane gales faced little resistance while blowing through the Popponessett forest in Mashpee. Pine trees were snapped off at fifteen to twenty feet off the ground. They weren't uprooted, "just snapped short as though a giant had been carelessly breaking matchsticks," according to the *Boston Globe*.

In Sandwich, the *Cape Cod Standard-Times* reported that the Coast Guard station's water tank at the post blew down and a small service vessel was sunk by the nine-foot tide. Wind speeds of seventy miles per hour were reported there.

The Chatham bridge out to Morris Island was swept away by the high tides. *Chapman family Loggia photo collection.*

In Chatham, boats were swept from the Stage Harbor shore and piled up on Terns Island. Alton Kenney's Marine Railway building collapsed, and the George Parker and George Crowell wharves, where the Stage Harbor fishing fleets tied up, were swept away.

Winds blew the steeple off the Chatham Universalist Church. Steve Chapman, whose family has owned the Loggia beach camp just south of Chatham Light since the late nineteenth century, has a photograph of the extensive damage done to the Morris Island bridge during the hurricane.

In Wellfleet, the Taylor Funeral Home was crushed by giant silver oak trees "likely brought here by a sea captain long ago," the *Boston Globe* said. Henry Carlson, who worked at the home, resided there with his wife and seven-year-old son. Fortunately for the Carlsons, there was no funeral going on, but fifteen empty coffins were ruined.

The Carlsons were at a reception that night and then returned home for coffee and sandwiches. When the first tree fell, the pantry door swung open, and it wouldn't shut again. They checked on their sleeping son, and his bed was shaking. Mrs. Carlson picked him up, and then the second falling tree took down the roof and wall.

In Provincetown, the morning of September 14 started quietly, but by mid-morning, the two square red flags were raised on High Pole Hill near the Pilgrim Monument. "They have a square black center, and they mean HURRICANE," the *Provincetown Advocate* said.

The Cape tip got off relatively easy compared to the rest of the peninsula during the 1938 hurricane, but this one proved to be more severe. The 1944 Hurricane "made the Hurricane of 1938 seem like a pleasant zephyr," the *Advocate* suggested. Wind gusts reached over one hundred miles per hour. "Through its howling could be heard the crashing of glass, the thud of falling bricks and the tearing of branches," the paper said.

The damage was widespread. The Atlantic House sign swung crazily and broke one of the big windows in Matta's store. A large downed tree completely blocked Center Street. Many windows were knocked out, including three in the New York Store. "Canned fruits and vegetables spilled into the street when the front window of the First National Store crashed," and "a tree in front of the library had been knocked down and the chimney had gone through the roof," the *Advocate* said.

After the 1938 storm, Provincetown was the subject of bogus news reports. The 1944 hurricane would produce more of the same, Cape-wide.

HURRICANE HOAXES

"More than 25,000 persons were homeless on Cape Cod," the *New York Herald Tribune* reported. The *Boston Herald* had this to say: "Part of Falmouth was without its normal water supply, but was being supplied by the Army from Camp Edwards." The Associated Press delivered this item: "Cape Codders were warned tonight not to touch any floating debris in the hurricane-struck area as it may contain explosives. State police relayed the warning over their teletype system at request of the Oceanographic Institution at Woods Hole." Within days, these reports were quickly debunked by the *Falmouth Enterprise*.

The *Boston Herald* reported that hotel and real estate interests feared that the Cape had been eliminated as a summer resort, with many seaside resorts being swept away. The *Enterprise* was quick to respond to the *Herald's* "defeatist point of view" on page one:

> *No Cape Cod hotel nor real estate interest suggested to the* Herald *that their neighborhood had been for a season eliminated as a summer resort. No Cape Codder told the* Herald *he feared Cape Cod houses might never be rebuilt. The* Herald *made it up. We dare say so because we know Cape Cod.*

The *Boston Post* also drew the ire of the *Provincetown Advocate* after declaring "Cape Tip Is Left in Ruins" and "Provincetown Placed Under Martial Law; Havoc Piles Up." The *Advocate* listed several of the items in the *Post*'s report, followed by the statement, "Not a single one of these statements is true," and then concluded its editorial: "In a time of severe and tragic stress such as we have just passed, it seems nothing less than a newspaper crime when a story is published, garbled and imaginary, which adds to the grief, worry and confusion of a situation which is already plenty bad enough."

The *Boston Globe* added a jab at its crosstown rival a few days later, saying, "If you'd like a good poke in the nose, just ask a Provincetown man if it is true they had 'martial law!'"

In the weeks following the storm, the cleanup project was on Cape-wide. Two hundred German prisoners of war, who were captured in the North African Campaign and detained at Camp Edwards on the Upper Cape, were assigned to building projects, farm work and, after the storm, harvesting fallen trees for lumber. According to *Images of America: Camp Edwards and Otis Air Force Base*, by Donald J. Cann and John Galluzzo, over eight million feet of lumber was salvaged by the prisoners under the supervision of the U.S. Army personnel knowledgeable of the industry. Four sawmills were set up at Camp Edwards.

The *Falmouth Enterprise* had praises for the Cape's preparedness for the storm after suffering so badly in 1938. "We have taken full force of a tropical hurricane right on the chin and weathered it," the *Enterprise* said. "News from Cape Cod is that it is seaworthy. Not even a hurricane can sink it." But Dennis historian Nancy Thacher Reid was quick to add in her book *Dennis, Cape Cod: From Firstcomers to Newcomers, 1639–1993*: "There had been no loss of human life. Still, we grieved."

HURRICANE CAROL

1954

The last century had four significant hurricanes all come within a sixteen-year period, and Carol and Edna came within twelve days of each other.
—Glenn Field, warning coordination meteorologist
at National Weather Service, Norton, Massachusetts, June 12, 2023

On the morning of August 31, 1954, the telephone rang at the home of John J. McLaughlin of Acapesket and Cumberland, Rhode Island. It was Martha Winick of Maravista calling, asking if his daughter Jean was available to babysit.

"An important engagement" was on their schedule, Winick said, according to a report in the *Falmouth Enterprise* four days later.

McLaughlin had much greater concerns on his mind. He had been monitoring weather reports all morning, growing concerned with the increasing waves coming off Vineyard Sound. Hurricane Carol, which had developed five days earlier in the Caribbean Sea, had rapidly intensified and was moving northward from North Carolina's Outer Banks, following a path eerily similar to the "Long Island Express" hurricane of 1938. A storm warning, covering Block Island, Rhode Island, to Portsmouth, New Hampshire, had been issued at 11:38 p.m. the previous evening, according to the *Cape Codder* newspaper of Orleans.

His daughter would not be babysitting that day. "Get out of the house," he warned Winick, but it was too late. Less than two hours later, Winick, along with her three daughters and sister Judge Golda Walters, had all perished when waves from the storm surge of Carol swept over Menahaunt Road and carried the Walters house "like a cork into Great Pond and smashed it to pieces," according to the *Enterprise*. A desperate last-minute effort at 11:00 a.m. by six men, lashed together with rope around their waists, to reach the Walters house failed. "Waves surged over the road shoulder high and stinging spray blinded the rescuers," the paper reported. The would-be rescuers, who included Arthur W. Corey, Reginald Campbell and Raleigh Costa, made it about one hundred yards but could go no farther.

Power had gone out shortly after Winick's phone call to McLaughlin, who would later aid in the rescue of two infants from a nearby house. Less than an hour later, a neighbor looked through the worsening weather conditions and saw a car standing in front of the house. "Those people are still there," she told her husband. "They can't be," he replied. At about eleven o'clock, they left to find safety.

Walters and her sister and her sister's children, ages seven, five and two, had spent two months in the beach cottage, known as the Ryder house.

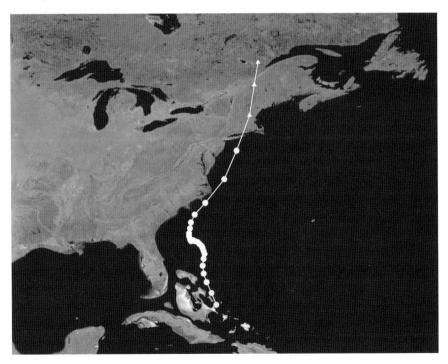

Hurricane Carol tracked over Central Massachusetts, leaving Cape Cod on the east side of the eye, where the highest winds were. *NOAA*.

Walters, the youngest woman ever appointed to a Massachusetts bench when she received her appointment in 1938, had suggested that she wanted to buy the house. They were among the seven lives lost on the Cape.

Carol was the first chapter of the late summer cyclonic onslaught. Another Hurricane Carol, which tracked just to the east of the Cape, had struck with less ferocity a year earlier, but it was the 1954 storm that would become the first Atlantic hurricane to have its name retired. Described by meteorologists as almost a twin to the 1938 Long Island Express, the Category 3 cyclone's storm surge coincided with high tide as it moved northward with a forward speed of forty miles per hour. The impact was felt Cape-wide, but once again, it was the communities along Nantucket Sound that were hardest hit. There was a storm surge of 14.0 feet, with sustained winds at eighty to one hundred miles per hour. William Winsor, a weather observer in Sandwich, recorded top wind speeds of ninety-eight miles per hour. High tide was 10.6 and 11.1 feet above mean high water on the Falmouth shore of Buzzards Bay. The lowest barometer reading checked in at 29.02 inches. Like the 1938 storm, Carol made its first landfall over Long Island and then again in Connecticut before the eye passed north through Central Massachusetts. In 2014, the *Cape Cod Times* reported that the storm affected 3,761 families and sent 2,500 people on the Cape to shelters. Half the Cape's homes lost power, which took a week to fully restore.

Walters and the Winicks weren't the only casualties of Carol, but like the 1944 hurricane, the death toll was significantly lower than 1938 thanks to the advance warnings and lessons learned from the earlier cyclone. Bourne registered one death, that of sixty-five-year-old Elmer Clapp, an invalid, who was drowned when his Taylor's Point cottage in Bourne was torn away and floated into the Cape Cod Canal.

The *Enterprise* told the story of how Elwell Perry and Joseph Kratz waded through waist-deep water to rescue two children from the Kemble house on Shore Road. Waterfront homes and the Robinson boat yard in Cataumet suffered severe flooding damage. Water swept over the causeway approaches to Wings Neck and Patuissett Island, sweeping them off their foundations. Several Patuissett houses ended up in the water, with one drifting up Buzzards Bay.

Water was waist-deep in the streets of Woods Hole. In the Penzance Point area, Rear Admiral Edward H. Smith, the Woods Hole oceanographic director, carried Mrs. Malcolm Park out of her flooded home on his shoulders and "got a woman off a boat seconds before an oil stove blew it up," the *Enterprise* said.

The Coast Guard vessel *Albatross* was tossed around the Woods Hole waterfront. *NOAA*.

Waves surged across Main Street into Eel Pond. Another foot of high tide would have claimed the research vessels of the Woods Hole Oceanographic Institute. The *Enterprise* told of a fuel tank breaking, spreading oil mixed with water into nearby houses. Another resident saw his coal bin and kerosene tank float away. The paper also reported on damage around the Fisheries, with the high seas wrecking every dock in the area and dragging the Coast Guard vessel *Albatross* "as far as the town dock."

The paper then added these two notes:

Seals at the Fisheries made their get-away about 10:30 a.m. Water carried them over the sea wall, and by noon covered even the wire fence that was mounted on the wall. Adding an ironical touch was a pamphlet floating down Millfield Street, which read "Be cheerful in the face of adversity."

In Bourne, twenty-year-old Donald Gerry nearly drowned when he tried to swim across a street to get home. Fighting a strong current caused by storm tides ten feet above normal and ninety-five-mile-per-hour winds crossing over the intersection of Bryant and Presidents Roads, he managed to hang on to a lamppost until someone could throw him a line and pull him to safety. "I don't know what in hell I had in mind," Gerry told the *Cape Cod Times* in August 1989. "I was afraid something was going to hit me."

A Woods Hole waterfront dock took a significant hit from Carol's high tides. *NOAA*.

David Webber was at Crosby's Landing in Osterville when the storm hit that morning. All was calm at 9:00 a.m., Webber told the *Times*, but by noon, boats were breaking free and coming ashore. The boat yard's main dock was lost in the storm.

The Lighthouse Inn on West Dennis Beach, which sustained serious damage in the 1944 hurricane, once again faced a terror of tropical origins. Carol "wiped out the downstairs area of the Inn, knocked the waterfront cottages off their foundations, and caused extensive damage," according to a historical dateline provided by the inn. The *Central Cape Press* reported that a DUKW vessel from the Chatham Coast Guard Station took fifteen people from the inn. Nearby Lower County Road and School Street experienced washouts.

The Stone family, owners of the inn, had their children taken to a Doric Avenue residence in Dennis. According to the Stones:

> *The children remembered that as they were leaving the Inn, one of the housekeepers, Alice was being blown across the front lawn. They screamed at her to get into the car, but she was quite deaf and the wind was howling. Finally the bellhop got out and led her to the car, and she was brought home*

to West Dennis center. The children eventually went to Nancy Sullivan's mother in law's house in Yarmouth, where they waited for their parents. The guests and employees were evacuated to Stoneleigh Gables. One guest refused to leave, and she was eventually carried out in her overstuffed armchair by waiters and bellhops and sent to Stoneleigh.

Across the road, the Sandbar, a local bar, was facing its own issues. As the Lighthouse Inn reported:

Jack Bumer, one of the bartenders from the Sandbar, spent the night at the Sandbar, sitting on top of the cases of liquor with a shotgun across his lap to prevent looters from taking the liquor. The bottles' labels were washed off, and the next night, the Sandbar opened for a hurricane party so guests could drink the "mystery" liquors.

The *Barnstable Patriot* reported no loss of life in its hometown, and building damage was less than in the previous hurricanes. However, boat damage was worse. Most "of the fleets of the Hyannis, Hyannisport, Wianno and Cotuit

Storm tides made their way into the lower levels of the Lighthouse Inn during Hurricane Carol. *Lighthouse Inn, West Dennis, Massachusetts.*

Yacht Clubs either sank at their moorings or were driven ashore," the *Patriot* said. Ocean Avenue, at the foot of Sea Street in Hyannis, and The Loop in Cotuit suffered extensive erosion damage. In the *Patriot*, a headline for a photograph page featuring boat damage read, "Cheer Up, It Was Worse in '44." Even the orange and blue Cape Cod Melody Tent was a casualty. "It was lowered to the ground when the canvas started to buckle," the *Patriot* said.

In South Yarmouth, "shore dwellers along Bass River and Vineyard Sound, where the water rose so fast it could be seen coming but car owners could get their parked cars out of range," the *Yarmouth Register* reported. Parker's River overflowed its banks and covered Route 28, surrounding Libby's Chowder House.

In Harwich Port, damage was heavy at Wychmere and Allen Harbor, where boats were torn from their moorings and dashed against the shore. The fire department had to rescue five men from the dredge in Wychmere Harbor after it tore loose from moorings. The Stone Horse Yacht Club float and boardwalk sustained damage, with several small sailboats overturned at their moorings.

In Chatham, boats were scattered about the Bridge Street end of Stage Harbor. The *Central Cape Press* also reported this Chatham oddity: "Debris topped by a 'No Parking—Driveway' sign littered the waterfront entrance to Harry Bearse's summer cottage, 'Good Anchorage,' at Stage Harbor."

Eastham's iconic windmill, first built in the seventeenth century, lost two of its arms. In Wellfleet, the high tides led to substantial flooding. Even though Provincetown was nearly sixty miles east of the hurricane's edge, Provincetown Airport manager John Van Arsdale reported winds of eighty-two miles per hour to the *Provincetown Advocate*.

"Hurricane Carol, which slapped Upper Cape Cod and other parts of New England hard, gave the Outer Cape only the back of its hand," wrote Frank Burling in the September 2, 1954 edition of the *Cape Codder*.

In Orleans, Phil Schwind, captain of the *White Cap* charter boat out of Rock Harbor, set off on a striped bass fishing trip with six Boston drugstore owners on Cape Cod Bay at 3:00 a.m. that morning. He wasn't aware of an impending hurricane until he called into the radio shack at Rock Harbor later, when Dickie Clark informed him of the forecast.

Schwind told the *Times* that he tried to head for cover in the Pamet River in Truro as conditions rapidly worsened. His party was calm until he told them to put life jackets on. He made it safely and said he never saw six men get off a boat so quickly. Schwind said it ruined the best fishing ever for bluefish: "The entire bay was like muddy soup. There wasn't a fish left in it."

One of the passengers had caught a striper earlier in the day before conditions worsened and had it mounted. The nameplate beneath the fish read: "Carol."

For Lydia (Moore) DuPertuis of Orleans, it was a rough experience, but not one of life-threatening proportions for the then-thirteen-year-old girl. Along with her aunt, two cousins and two friends, she went out for a camping trip to Sampson Island in Pleasant Bay and rode out the storm before being rescued by the Coast Guard. "Weathermen had been watching Carol for days and her antics had been unusual and deceiving," the *Provincetown Advocate* reported in its September 2, 1954 edition.

Yet that didn't seem to bother Charles Moore, who gave his daughter the OK to camp out in the storm. The Moores, who lived on a farm in Wayland, Massachusetts, loved stormy weather, often taking in thunderstorms from the family's screened porch. In a 2018 interview, DuPertuis recalled: "We knew the storm was coming, and we asked my father, and he said, 'No, go ahead!' There was six of us and Patty, a mixed breed dog. We pitched tents, ate, and everything, and then the storm hit sometime during the night. I don't remember being scared a bit."

Boat damage was extensive in Pleasant Bay. Many trees came down, and streets were littered with limbs and leaves. Power was out for fourteen hours the next day, but phone service was available in most parts of the Outer Cape even at the height of the storm.

The next day, three young men—Steve Bartow, Bobby Gesner and Ron Sveden—were the first to attempt a rescue. Bartow told the *Cape Codder*:

Mr. Sprague at Howard Johnson's told me this morning that the girls were out on Sampson's. So the three of us went down to Nauset Beach in my beach buggy to see if we could help them. We waded and swam across the shallow waters on the eastern side of the island. We got to the island we checked to see that everyone was all right. Then we walked their boat around to the lee shore but decided not to try to ferry them across because the tide was coming in and the winds were getting worse.

DuPertuis added: "Those three boys came to rescue us, and that wasn't enough. Steve Bartow wanted to get us out and they realized that it wasn't safe. My father sent the Coast Guard."

The Coast Guard dispatched the DUKW, or "Duck," to the island from "Old Field Point, near the home of the Francis W. Sargents," according to the *Cape Codder*. In command was William Joseph, along with Herman

Benton and Robert Bruno. Also on board were Harbormaster Elmer Darling, auxiliary policeman Whit Scott Jr. and Fire Chief Larry Ellis.

Taken off the island, in addition to the three older boys, in the heavy wind and rain were DuPertuis; her aunt Mabel Nichols and her two daughters, True and Cathy; Jane MacPherson; and Ann Beibly. DuPertuis recalled, "When we got off the boat, we were completely wet, and the boys gave us some of their clothes to wear. I remember wearing an old Army shirt, and there were just crowds there on the beach. It was like, 'Oh, what is this?!'"

The *Cape Codder* reported that Cathy Nichols was told that she was "a lucky duck" for getting a ride in the amphibious vehicle. "Yes, spelled DUKW," was her reply. Mabel Nichols, clutching Patty the dog, wasn't as enthusiastic about the experience. "This is awful," she told the *Cape Codder*. "We've been planning this camping trip for seven years and this had to happen." "A friend of ours was visiting from Connecticut," DuPertuis added. "I can't imagine what her family thought!"

Overall, Carol was a tropical nightmare for the Cape, but for DuPertuis, her memories of this memorable weather event were a little more "pleasant" than most. "We were well prepared, I thought," she said. "We had blankets, food, a tent, a dog—what more could you want?"

Twelve days later, Cape Cod would end up getting more of what it didn't want—another unwelcome visitor from the tropics that went by the name of Edna.

HURRICANE EDNA

1954

*I had just left the bridge when the hurricane hit with a thunderous roar.
This is it, I thought.
Abandon ship? No, if the* Nantucket *had sunk, we would have gone with
her. Our boats were swept away.*
—*Chief Boatswain's Mate John C. Corea of Provincetown, skipper of the
lightship* Nantucket, *Associated Press, September 1954*

During the morning hours of September 12, 1954, the area around Cape Cod and the Islands was bracing for the second tropical cyclone lashing in two weeks, as Hurricane Edna had Martha's Vineyard and Falmouth in its crosshairs. No land dwellers in the area would perish from this storm, despite its winds of ninety to one hundred miles per hour. Forty-nine miles south of Nantucket, the twelve-man crew of the *Nantucket/* LV-112 Lightship Station were very close to being lost in the raging seas, experiencing what the crew called "two hours of hell." The Associated Press report of September 16, 1954, reported: "The 959-ton floating lighthouse, her bow plates smashed, her rudder gone and her bridge almost demolished, groped into port under tow. 'Aboard was the 12-man crew who couldn't have abandoned ship—even if they wanted to.'"

At the time, the *Nantucket* lightship was the largest lightship in the world, according to a report in the *Falmouth Enterprise*, but was nearly no match for what Edna was about to throw its way. According to *The Fog Horn*, the newsletter of the U.S. Coast Guard Lightship Sailors Association, in 2011, Richard Arnold of Gloucester was on watch, with the ship "bobbing up

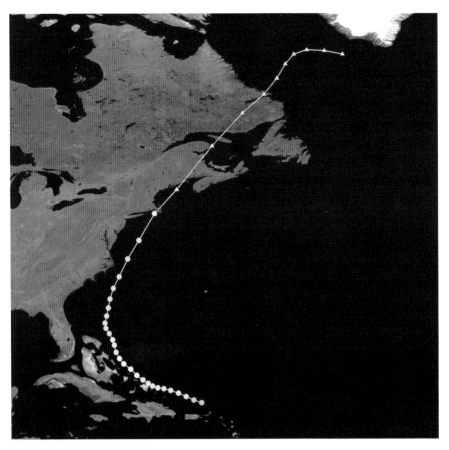

Twelve days after Hurricane Carol pounded New England, Hurricane Edna tracked over Cape Cod, causing more damage. *NOAA.*

and down." Richard recalled "a mountain of 'green water' approaching in the distance which appeared to be sixty or seventy feet high, traveling at an extremely fast pace." He attempted to summon Chief Boatswain's Mate John C. Corea of Provincetown, the lightship's commanding officer, but the wave struck the ship and smashed through the three-quarter-inch portholes. The ship suffered major damage to the hull and lost power and the ability to steer after the lightship's anchor chain broke from its mooring. The *Falmouth Enterprise* reported this account from Coast Guard officials: "One big wave boiled over the ship, caved in six portholes, poured into the engines and carried off both boats and the life raft."

With the crew sloshing their way through the water that the ship was taking on, fuse panels, switches and radio equipment began to malfunction.

On the radio, Jim Sheahan of Yarmouth was trying to send out an SOS, with sparks flying from the radio. "Any acknowledgement of the distress signal was lost in the mountainous seas," according to the Associated Press. Two and a half hours later, Sheahan got off another message: "We're taking a helluva beating."

According to the AP, the cutters *Yakutat* and *Campbell* steamed to their aid. A Coast Guard reconnaissance plane flew out of New York, and from Woods Hole, the buoy tender *Hornbeam* rushed to the *Nantucket*'s assistance at 3:53 p.m. The *Nantucket* was eventually towed to Boston.

After the rescue, observers marveled at how the *Nantucket* crew survived, unlike the crew of the *Vineyard* lightship ten years earlier. As Arnold told the AP, "What did I do? Man, I prayed—I prayed real hard."

Hurricane Edna was the second of the twin hurricanes of 1954, following a similar but slightly more eastward track than Carol. Even though Edna was the less severe of the two Category 3 cyclones, most of Cape Cod lost power. A six-foot storm surge and a rising tide destroyed boats from one end of the Cape to the other, and aided by heavy erosion from Carol, the landscapes of beaches suffered as well. Abnormally low barometer readings, lower than the previous hurricanes, were recorded at Bass River (28.16), Chatham (28.2) and Yarmouth Port (28.3).

In West Dennis, the Lighthouse Inn's main building was heavily flooded once again. According to the inn's hurricane exhibit, on display in the building's lower level:

> *Two guests had asked to have their cars stored in the garage where they knocked against the walls and doors, and were flooded with six feet of water. Cars in the parking lot didn't fare any better. According to Bob Stone, a waiter and busboy in 1953 and '54, the Inn stayed open after Carol but closed after Edna, when there was no electricity. Bob said he and his brother were the only two employees who stayed to work, working three meals a day, seven days a week, which was the normal schedule anyway. Bob said the two employee dorms were flooded, and the houses all floated off their foundations. He said he rode his bike up town to call his parents and tell them he was OK, but the telephone service wasn't working.*

According to the *Falmouth Enterprise*'s reports from the National Weather Service, Edna centered over Martha's Vineyard at 1:45 p.m. and at about 3:00 p.m. passed close to Falmouth. The wind was almost calm by 3:30 p.m. and rose again to gale force at 4:00 p.m., with the storm concluding about an hour later. The National Weather Service later determined that Edna was "a less severe storm at its center," according to the *Enterprise*:

> *The East Boston weather bureau said reports appear to sustain the interpretation that Edna separated into two centers. If it did, the bureau scientists say, the two centers or eyes were very close together. The backlash of the passing storm was more severe here than the approaching wind. Through the first phase the wind was southeast. In the backlash the wind veered to northwest.*

Another oddity was the tides. The *Enterprise* reported that high tides in West Falmouth came only seven hours apart. Low tide for Falmouth Harbor was due at 4:18 p.m., but "water was lapping at the level of the town landing" a half hour earlier. Then, "it turned suddenly and appeared to drop a foot in ten minutes."

The tide table went by the boards Saturday. Low tide for Falmouth harbor was due at 4:18 p.m. A half hour before that, water was lapping at the level of the town landing. It turned suddenly and appeared to drop a foot in ten minutes.

The *Barnstable Patriot* reported a similar extreme in their hometown. A photographer captured the calm at Ocean Street in Hyannis at 3:30 p.m., but an hour later, boat owners at Crosby's Landing in Osterville were "watching their cruisers and yachts being buffeted by ninety mile-per-hour winds."

Most forecasts had the worst of the storm passing by early afternoon, according to the *Patriot*, but when the hurricane-force winds returned later, "we realized that the second phase or backlash of Edna was doing its dirty work." Parts of the Outer Cape saw similar situations. Glenn Field, the warning coordination meteorologist at the Boston National Weather Service in Norton, Massachusetts, summarized Edna's odd behavior during a June 2023 interview:

> *Massachusetts is the only place I think that has this issue, maybe in the world, because of the shape of Cape Cod. It's the only place that can get the maximum storm surge after the hurricane leaves. This is when Edna passed over the Cape and out to sea, at this location (near Stellwagen Bank) the winds turn northwest behind it, and that's where it piles into the inner portion of Cape Cod Bay and Wellfleet Harbor. So the maximum storm surge of ten feet in Wellfleet Harbor occurs an hour and a half after the eye reached the south side of the Cape. It's not a "one size fits all" around here.*

THE BLIZZARD OF '78

*To me, it was the greatest weather event that I'd ever witnessed on the Cape,
and remains so to this day…in terms of its scale, and how it affected the
community, and the culture.*
—Bob Seay, January 2008

During the early morning hours of February 7, 1978, news reporter
Bob Seay of WVLC radio in Orleans was on the phone, checking in
with the police departments of the Outer Cape Cod towns. One of his first
calls went to the Eastham Police Department.

"Oh, my God!" the Eastham dispatcher said. "You would not believe
Coast Guard Beach!"

"What do you mean?" Seay replied.

"You should just get down there," the dispatcher said. "Everything's
washed away."

A ferocious northeaster had swept over southeastern New England
during the night. To the northwest, Boston was in the middle of a record-
setting snowstorm, and the Upper Cape region saw close to a foot of
accumulation. Across the Outer Cape, the storm began as snow the
previous afternoon but turned to rain overnight. The storm would forever
be known in most places as the infamous Blizzard of '78, but with the high
winds and high tides on the Cape, it was more like "the great tidal event of
'78," Seay said in a 2008 interview.

High storm tides overran Coast Guard Beach in Eastham during the storm of February 6–7, 1978. *Cape Cod National Seashore.*

Seay jumped in his car and headed for Coast Guard Beach, a barrier spit of sand along the Cape Cod National Seashore that may best be known as the site of author Henry Beston's "Outermost House." What Bob saw upon his arrival left him stunned:

> *All I could see was this ocean that seemed to have just grown in size, literally. It wasn't the waves, it was the tide…the actual size of the ocean. It was so huge. And it was washing right to the south of the Coast Guard station there. It was something that the old timers had kind of anticipated for a long time, because they had seen that area when it had dunes going out a quarter of a mile or so, and now it had completely eroded. All of these houses that were out there were just wrecked and washed away. I couldn't see down to the "Outermost House," but that was just one of several structures that seemed to be gone.*

The storm gave "people enough to talk about for the next hundred years," recalled the January 2, 1979 edition of the *Cape Codder.* "It arrived, Monday, February 6, roaring onto Cape Cod like a gigantic steam roller. By the time it moved offshore Tuesday night it had carved a place in the history books." The storm destroyed the Coast Guard Beach parking lot, produced record high sea levels, started a nasty pattern of the Atlantic breaking through the dunes of Ballston Beach into the Pamet River in Truro, cut off Eastham from Orleans during high tide, destroyed several beach camps and left a Volkswagen swamped in Nauset Marsh.

The now-infamous weather system, which buried eastern Massachusetts in three to four feet of snow and changed the landscape of the Outer Cape's beaches forever, first developed a few days earlier in the Gulf of Mexico. The extra-tropical cyclone was a slow mover at first, according to the *Cape Codder*:

> *The whole mess started with two storms. One came in from the west and another from the south. They merged off Cape Hatteras and started moving north as one, according to records at the U.S. Weather Station in Chatham. The storm was about 500 miles across. It traveled slowly, covering only 200 miles in 24 hours.*

The storm, which was blocked by a cold high-pressure area to the north, was in a position to send band after band of heavy snow across southeastern Massachusetts. Meanwhile, a storm surge that was estimated to be three to four feet over the regular high tide combined with the abnormally high tides from the new moon. During the previous month, Wallace Bailey of the Massachusetts Audubon Society's Wellfleet Bay Wildlife Sanctuary had circled the high tide dates of February 6 and 7 on his calendar, noted Nan Turner in her book *Journey to Outermost House*. Eastham historian Noel Beyle recalled in a 2008 interview how it all played out: "It was an unusual event, because you had a lot of things happening at the same time. You had a nor'easter coming up the coast, and it stalled over the Cape. It actually had an eye, and the sun came out the day after. It also occurred at the time of a very, very high astronomical tide."

The *Cape Codder* noted that winds gusted to ninety-two miles per hour at the U.S. Weather Service Station in Chatham, along with a low barometer reading of 29.34 inches. The new moon tides caused sea levels to rise four feet above normal. That historic tide rearranged Coast Guard Beach, transforming what, in the 1920s, was a towering barrier beach of dunes nearly three miles long and a quarter of a mile wide. Thanks largely to this storm, Coast Guard Beach became a flattened-out sand spit that is, as of 2023, a little over a mile long and perhaps one hundred yards wide.

Yet the February storm of 1978 didn't do it alone. It actually had some help from another storm that occurred in January, Waldron recalled during a 1991 interview for the Cape Cod Writers Center program "Books and the World":

You could see that the dunes were being eaten away, and from a distance, that the height of the dunes was lowering. So it was just a matter of time before the ultimate storm arrived. The storm in January of 1978 sort of set the stage for a major storm to move in, because it wiped out the sand bars off Nauset Beach.

Jack Clarke, a twenty-six-year-old Cape Cod National Seashore ranger at that time, also voiced concern after the January storm, as he recalled in a 2008 interview: "That January storm almost took out everything at Coast Guard Beach. There was a lot of moisture and dampness in the dunes and in the beach itself. That storm came very close to the kind of destruction that we saw in February."

"One big storm per winter is average, Waldron added. "So everyone relaxed as January came to an end—everyone except the professional weather forecasters."

The elimination of those sandbars, so cherished by many a surfer over the years, would prove to be the nail in the coffin. Even though the January storm struck during a period of low tides, Conrad Nobili, owner of the Butterfly House cottage on Nauset Spit, noted the change in the sandbars. "Conrad…was well aware that Nauset was on borrowed time," Waldron wrote in *Journey to Outermost House*. "Still, it could be years."

However, it would be only a matter of days. "By February 6, 7, and 8, the beach was vulnerable," Clarke said. The monster winter hurricane and its astronomical high tides flattened out Nauset Spit and washed away eight of its beach camps.

The January storm also put the public on alert. As the National Oceanic and Atmospheric Administration noted in a natural disaster survey report later that year, the January "storm had sensitized the public and agencies to the threat posed by major winter storms."

During the winter months, Clarke stayed at the Nauset Lightkeeper's house. Miriam Rowell, who owned the house from 1957 to 1982, wintered in London and enlisted Clarke to housesit for her. After a rough ride home from the Salt Pond Visitors Center, he spent one of the most memorable nights of his life in that house, as he recalled in 2008: "Anyone who has that Cape Cod license plate, or gets a bag of Cape Cod Potato Chips, will see that keeper's house and the window facing the ocean. Well, that was my bedroom that night in a big brass bed."

Clarke and his brother Danny and some friends had "a little storm party" that evening. "I noticed that the water in the toilet was starting to wave as the northeast wind picked up off the ocean," Clarke recalled in 2023. "Danny noticed the same in his beer mug. The place was rocking." When Danny tried to leave later on, his car "door almost blew off, bending its hard steel hinges and refusing to shut." He eventually made it home safely later.

The snow turned to rain after midnight, Clarke recalled. "It seemed like there was warm, tropical air offshore mixing with all that humidity and precipitation." Any snow that fell was gone by morning. However, the hurricane-force gusts began battering the house, which had been recently re-shingled. That was just the beginning, Clarke recalled:

> *That night, the shingles just blew off the house, and water poured into the second floor, all the way down through the stairs. We had a major flood. I was not only afraid of some really serious destruction of the house from the wind; I thought the whole window and frame was going to blow in. So I just pulled the covers over me and it was like there was a ghost in the room. The paperback books flew all around the room and fine, silt sand just blew in the window, and the back of the room had a little sand dune at the bottom of the floor.*

Outside the house was even worse. Electricity went out everywhere, with blue flashes all along the wires on Ocean View Drive from Nauset Light down to Coast Guard Beach. In his 2008 interview, Clarke described the elemental fury: "One of the most impressive things outside of watching the ocean was the sound of the wind, and the wind blowing between the house and the lighthouse. If you actually got down on the beach on the sixth, it was a deafening roar, with the ground itself shaking with each wave."

In 2023, Clarke added more details about his near-sleepless night:

> *A deep sleep was out of the question. My mind raced. Was there anyone else living this close to the edge of the raging sea tonight? Should I even be staying here? Even Danny earlier questioned the wisdom of riding out the storm at the Light. But this house has withstood a century-and-a-half of storms even though it was already moved back from the edge of the eroding cliff once before. Did I have a choice now? What if the erosion at the bottom of the cliff brings the house sliding down into the ocean? I was not ready for a Dorothy-like "Wizard of Oz" tornado ride.*

As the storm began on February 6, Henry Lind, Eastham's natural resources officer, took a ride down Coast Guard Beach a couple of hours prior to high tide to evaluate the situation. Wash-overs on the beach were becoming more common over the years, but this storm was taking it to a new level, he recalled in a 2008 interview:

I probably was the last person that drove back in off that trail before the storm. I made through that one spot, and looked back, and two or three more waves put several feet of water through that area, and it was no longer passable. The storm continued to develop through the day, and at sunset, it was raging.

As the storm continued on Monday night, four young people crammed into a blue 1964 Volkswagen Beetle and made their way into the Coast Guard Beach parking lot to watch the wild weather. The next morning, Seay noticed the VW floating in the marsh and later tracked down its occupants, who managed to escape a harrowing experience. The newsman recalled:

They thought, "Wouldn't it be neat to drive down to Coast Guard Beach and see the storm?" This was a storm of tremendous magnitude. They decided to go down there in the dark. The problem was, when they entered the parking lot, in their headlights, they couldn't see any water, but what they didn't realize is that the waves were breaking behind them. So all of a sudden, they're driving down the parking lot, and this wave lifts this Volkswagen up in the air; their lights go out. The Beetle comes back down into the parking lot; they try to open the doors, there's swirls of water. They're up to their waists in water. The rain, they said, felt like bullets; the wind was so strong. The only thing that saved their lives was that they looked up on the hill, and there was a car parked by the Coast Guard station with its headlights on. They literally crawled their way up the bank to that car. Without those headlights, they believed they would have perished.

"The car was hit from behind by a wave. It started to spin us around and then we started floating down the parking lot," Gary Carpenter, the owner of the VW, told the *Cape Cod Times* in 1998.

Once in the parking lot, the foursome noticed a Ford Triumph approaching the beach. They began shouting in the direction of the Triumph, whose two occupants thought the voices were coming from the about-to-be submerged VW. Down to the parking lot the Triumph went—it, too, was swamped by waves, stranding the vehicle, although not in nearly as much danger as the VW was. The Triumph "suffered no ill effects," according to the *Cape Codder*.

Storm tides swept an occupied Volkswagen Beetle into Eastham's Nauset Marsh. The occupants managed to escape. *Cape Cod National Seashore.*

Henry Beston's Outermost House floats through Nauset Marsh after storm tides swept the author's cottage off its foundation. *Eastham Historical Society.*

Nan Turner Waldron, author of the book *Journey to Outermost House*, sits on the steps of Henry Beston's Outermost House after the cottage was flooded in May 1977. *Author's collection.*

John Brown, the co-owner of Brownie's Texaco in Orleans, towed the VW out of the marsh on Tuesday, and all of its fluids were changed. On Wednesday, February 8, the key to the VW was turned at 12:07 p.m. "Damned if the thing didn't start!" Seay chuckled. "Volkswagen should have been there for their commercial!"

On Tuesday morning, after Seay witnessed what was going on at Coast Guard Beach, he rushed back to the Salt Pond Visitors Center to phone in a report to the radio station. "Within minutes, you could see the cars start to come down to the beach," he said.

OUTERMOST HOUSE DESTROYED

Eight cottages, including Henry Beston's Outermost House, were swept off their foundations. Clarke was in the cupola of the Eastham Coast Guard station and witnessed the iconic cottage being lifted off its posts by the incoming tide. Splintered remains of Beston's house, which were featured in a *Cape Codder* photograph with Lind and Conrad Nobili, were recovered at Fort Hill and in East Orleans. Another cottage that was swept away was Nobili's Butterfly House, which was captured on film from the air by pilot

Storm waves overcome the Coast Guard Beach bathhouse on February 7, 1978. *Cape Cod National Seashore.*

Richard Kelsey. Nobili's Butterfly House, an architectural marvel designed by its owner, was built on the dunes during the 1960s. As longtime Eastham resident Tommy Dill, who served in the Coast Guard during the 1950s and later operated Jasper's Surf Shop, the first of its kind on Cape Cod, in Eastham with Mike Houghton, noted in 2016: "It was all glass in the front. In the afternoons, when the sun was shining on it, it would light up, like it was on fire, from the reflection off the glass windows. It looked like the place was burning up."

By Tuesday, the potent weather system had begun to stall and developed an "eye." The *Cape Codder* described the unique scene:

> On Tuesday morning, Cape Codders were treated to a breath of spring for several hours. The wind died, the temperature rose and the sun shone brightly down on those who ventured out to inspect the damage of the night before. It was an oasis of calm moving slowly over the peninsula. In Boston, the snow was still falling in the afternoon.

Historian Noel Beyle admitted in 2008 that on the first night of the storm, he wasn't all that concerned while sitting in his bayside home. "Just a lot of wind," he said. The next morning, his phone rang:

"Hey, have you been out yet?"

"No."

"Why don't you go over to Coast Guard Beach? There's a lot of interesting stuff happening over there. The Coast Guard Beach bathhouse is being slammed by waves."

Beyle grabbed his camera and gear and headed to the beach. He recalled his adventure in a 2008 interview:

Seventeen rolls later, standing out in the driveway, taking pictures of that beach bathhouse getting absolutely clobbered. There was only one guy who was a complete idiot to go out there. Everybody else was up on the bluff, but I went down into the driveway and put the camera on a tripod and shot and shot and shot, hoping for the right shot…and I did!

Clarke recalled during those 2008 interviews that the two ends of the bathhouse washed away during that night. By morning, only the main core of the building, a hexagon, remained. It still stood but was no longer safe, and Seashore rangers had no choice but to burn down what was left of the structure.

Beyle described the storm as "a monumental event" but saw a bright side with the arrival of the eye:

Down here, we didn't have any snow or anything like that. Boston got absolutely clobbered, just clobbered—they had two or three feet of snow. While we're watching all this stuff on the tube about what's going on in Boston, we're saying, "Boston? Where's that? I mean, that's not even in the ballpark! It's nice, the sun's out…ready to get your trunks on and go swimming!"

RECORD HIGH TIDES

The high tides reached record levels, Dr. Graham Giese of the Center for Coastal Studies in Provincetown told the *Cape Codder*. Giese, an oceanographer who specializes in tides and sea levels, spent the storm "taking measurements every ten minutes on the pier in Provincetown," he said in a 2023 interview. "It was the most I've ever measured." At the height of the storm surge, there was no wind. "There were high water levels on the bay and in the dunes near Beach Point," Giese marveled. "You could see water seeping up from below, just water everywhere."

During those high tides, "Route 6…was covered [by] salt water twice in Eastham at a dip in the road near Fort Hill," the *Cape Codder* said. The highway was covered with two to four inches at high tide around 11:00 p.m. on Monday, followed by an even higher amount the next morning, when six to eight inches covered the road. As Clarke recalled, "Down at the end of Fort Hill, the entire marsh system washed out. There was actually water connecting the ocean and the bay at the bottom of Fort Hill. You actually couldn't get down from Eastham to Orleans. It was cut off during the high tide."

Tom King of the state DPW was directing traffic at the site during the Tuesday morning high tides. "Twelve or thirteen years ago," King responded when asked by the *Cape Codder* about when he thought the last water covered Route 6. "I probably won't see it again either." Many cars were out on the road during Tuesday's balmy weather. "Take it easy," King told motorists as they were working their way through the water. "These people think this is fresh water. They don't know that it's salt water that can damage their cars."

At Collins Cove near the rotary, high tides flooded the inside of the Collins cottage colony's Shucking House. Eastham fire chief John Hilferty told the *Cape Codder* that the tides flooded sections of Bridge, Ellis and Samoset Roads, with the worst of it at Governor Prence Road. As the *Cape Codder* noted, "Two Cape Codders were seen traveling that road by the only means possible: canoe." Tuesday's high tide brought water over the Ballston Beach parking lot, over Pamet Head and into the Pamet River. Truro town clerk Tom Kane said he watched a photographer set up his tripod on a dune next to the parking lot and become swamped in waist-deep water as he was taking photos with his back to the ocean, according to the *Cape Codder*.

Water levels reached over the piers at Rock Harbor and Wellfleet Harbor. Bayside roads were flooded. Fortunately, this tide came during the calm period. Had there even been a thirty-mile-per-hour wind kicking up five-foot waves, "that would have been a disaster for Provincetown and parts of Truro," Giese said.

The *Cape Codder* went into great detail explaining the details of the record sea levels:

> *High tide was 14.5 feet above the current mean low water level. A normal average spring high tide for Provincetown would be 10.6 feet above mean*

low water. A twelve-foot tide is considered quite high. The high tide was caused by two coincidental events. The first was the storm; a low pressure area causes a long wave called a "storm surge" on the surface of the sea. High tide itself is a very long wave. The elevation of the water surface moves along at the same speed as the low pressure area. The other force on the tide was the "new moon" Tuesday. It exerts the same pull on the tides as a full moon; the moon and sun are lined up on the same side of the earth.

"The tide was not caused by the waves, Dr. Giese said, and for Provincetown and other parts of the coast, this was just 'incredibly lucky.'" Nature wasn't all to blame for the tide having such easy access to Coast Guard Beach, Seay explained in the 2008 interview:

There had been erosion there in previous years, and the National Seashore had decided to take all this concrete from the Army base in South Wellfleet and dump it right in front of the Coast Guard station to try and halt the erosion. It was a disastrous decision. Not only did it make it a very unpleasant place to go with all these rocks there, it really didn't stop the erosion that much, but what it did do was weaken the area to the south, which would starve the area of the sand it would get, and this would pave the way for the break that would happen. The Seashore would later go back and spend $100,000 trying to remove all of that concrete.

DEVASTATION ON THE DUNES

Along Provincetown's back shore, the rustic dune shacks were facing their share of elemental challenges from the historic storm. Nat and Mildred Champlin were at their Mission Bell dune shack during the Christmas season of 1977 when Mildred noticed that their shack's frontage had dwindled over the past few years from "a gentle slope of 210 feet of beach grass to an alarmingly steep cliff about 25 feet high, just about 30 feet or so from the front of our house. The erosion was progressing at a worrying pace, but it looked OK that Christmas, so we felt a little reassured," she noted in a 2023 correspondence.

The Champlins returned to their home in Michigan but received a phone call when the storm hit the Cape, informing them of the damage on the dunes of Provincetown. Their neighbor on the dunes, Leo Fleurant, had

The Adams shack on the dunes of Provincetown is pushed back on to the dunes following extensive damage during the February 1978 storm. *Cape Cod National Seashore.*

Leo Fleurant's dog, Wrinkles, gazes at the sharp drop-off from the eroded sands under the Adams shack on the dunes of Provincetown following the February 1978 storm. Fleurant's shack escaped unharmed. *Cape Cod National Seashore.*

moved his shack back off the dune a month earlier. Fleurant and his dog, Wrinkles, had come through the storm in good shape, but the neighboring Adams shack wasn't as fortunate. It was hanging on the edge of the dune and required the services of Pinky Silva and his local construction business to save the structure. Utilizing two bulldozers, a couple of trucks, some other equipment, some I-beams and five or six men, Silva managed to get the shack out of harm's way. Mildred Champlin offered this description of the overall scene in a 2023 correspondence:

> *The storm's damage changed our landscape in a major way. No longer did we have the gentle slope down to the water we had in the 50's and 60's that a town artist likened to a beautiful wheat field, but were left perched on a jagged primary dune whose terrain changed with every wind, eroding in the most unexpected ways. We did eventually gain as much as 125 feet of grassland in front of the houses, which encouraged us to think we might be OK after all.*

Up until November 1977, North Beach in Chatham was home to the Old Harbor Life-Saving Station, constructed there in 1896. With high tides regularly threatening the structure, it was moved by barge to Provincetown Harbor, where it would ride out the storm and suffer minimal damage. The remaining buildings from the Old Harbor station were destroyed by the storm.

North Beach, covered by water at one point, was breached by the ocean in four places. "Some cottages were flooded, others were gone, some were turned over, split in half," the *Cape Cod Chronicle* reported. According to the *Register*, eight of the thirty-eight beach camps there suffered some structural or water damage. One of the twelve camps in Orleans was moved from its foundation, and one of the nine camps on Monomoy Island was destroyed.

George Costa's North Beach camp wasn't washed away but was buried by sand. According to Costa's account of the storm in *Drifting Memories: The Nauset Beach Camps on Cape Cod*, by Frances L. Higgins, access to the cabin was impossible. "The level of sand was the same inside as it was outside," Costa noted. "There was no way of digging it out and restoring it." Costa eventually had to burn the camp and rebuild. The Truelove Camp was washed off its foundation, but they moved it back to its original spot.

The *Chronicle* reported that the wreck of the *Pendleton* off Monomoy Island, stuck in the water since the 1952 disaster, broke apart. In Chatham, Bridge Street began flooding as the tide neared its crest midday. Old Mill Boat Road, the Morris Island dike and Ryders Cove Landing were being inundated. The *Chronicle* described the overall post-storm scene in Chatham: "At noon, hundreds stood on the heights west of Chatham Harbor and Pleasant Bay and watched the Atlantic pour across, smashing some cottages, flooding others. The waters guzzled into any low-lying areas. Where Old Harbor station had been, there was only ocean."

Chatham town and police officials flew over the area Tuesday afternoon in a Nauset Airways plane. "It was like flying over a wasteland," Selectman Edward Harrington said. "Cottages were split, toppled, washed away— there was waste everywhere." The ocean also tore through Monomoy Island at Hammonds Bend, where it had broken two years earlier.

The shoreline disasters that occurred in the Boston area prompted immediate response from Chatham. Contacted by Salvation Army headquarters in Boston, Harrington Jack M. Hammett put the word out over local radio and made arrangements for an appeal for food and clothing. Within forty-nine hours, a Salvation Army official was in Chatham to pick up an estimated one thousand pounds of clothing and food.

One of the surviving Nauset Spit beach camps was still standing as of the fall of 2023. The Dill beach camp is now safely tucked away in the confines of the Eastham Historical Society's Swift-Daley House complex after it was moved off the beach in 1980. Tommy Dill, whose family owned the camp, had this recollection in June 2016: "I have an article from a couple of weeks after the storm, from the *Cape Codder*, and it shows the house standing up on the dunes and the ocean swirling all around it. It wasn't even on a high dune, it was on a low dune, but for some reason, the ocean just went right around it."

Warren Quinn of Orleans moved the house off its eroding dune to the Coast Guard Beach parking lot before Bill Hoffman completed the transition to the Dills' Eastham property. There it sat for two years before Don Sparrow convinced Dill to donate the cottage to the Eastham Historical Society.

How did it survive? Dill gives credit to the pilings under the shack, which reached fourteen feet down into the sand. "Thank goodness, it's still there," Dill concluded. "Just by luck, everything turned out OK."

The storm made its biggest impact on the eastern third of the peninsula: "The only real damage was on the outer shore, Provincetown to Monomoy," the *Cape Cod Chronicle* said. In 2008, Clarke insisted that this storm's impact will never be forgotten: "There's a lot of hysteria on the news now when we get, you know, 'rain with wind,' and they have 'Storm Force' advisories and all that. This is the barometer that all storms will be measured with in our lifetime. I'm convinced of that. There haven't been any storms to compare with it."

THE 1987 JANUARY NORTHEASTER

It was seismic for this town.
—Jeffrey Dykens on the Chatham Bar break of 1987,
as told to the Cape Cod Chronicle, *January 4, 2017*

On the afternoon of Friday, January 2, 1987, a ferocious winter storm was raging over Cape Cod. At the Chatham Coast Guard station, overlooking Chatham Harbor and the barrier beach that had been protecting it from the Atlantic Ocean for centuries, there was about to be a major change in the lay of the land.

An abnormally high tide, powered by a number of elemental forces, was in the process of making Cape Cod history. Chatham Bar had experienced "the breakthrough." Petty Officer Bob St. Pierre of the Chatham Coast Guard Station was on duty and relayed what he saw to the *Cape Cod Times*: "It's two hours after high tide, and she's still barreling through there. She's really blown apart; there are really tremendous seas—fifteen-foot, eighteen-foot seas anyhow—and it's just plain washing through."

The northeaster came calling nearly nine years after another life-changing storm, the Blizzard of '78. This system was delivering wind gusts of sixty-eight miles per hour, along with an eight- to twelve-foot storm surge and a rare celestial alignment known as "syzygy." In the words of the *Boston Globe*, "The term describes a celestial lineup of Earth, moon and sun when the moon aligns directly opposite the Earth and sun or between the two bodies. The alignment bulges the tides in some areas of the earth."

Chatham Bar, as shown in 1986, before the northeaster of January 2, 1987. *NASA.*

The storm quickly made its mark on the new cut. According to the *Cape Codder*, photographer Richard Kelsey and Chatham Airport manager Dan Wolfe flew over the area that weekend and reported "channels began forming in the cut-through." While many believed the cut would eventually close, that wasn't the case. On February 10, Dr. Graham Giese of the Center for Coastal Studies in Provincetown provided this account to the *Cape Codder*:

We already know the inlet has grown. On January 16, one hour after high tide, the inlet measured 405 feet across. On February 3, at an hour and a half before high tide, it measured 1,620 feet. Erosion has occurred along the northern tip of the newly created "south" beach, while the southern tip of North Beach has extended somewhat further south.

In a 2023 interview, Giese described the cyclical pattern of change in the barrier beach system off Chatham and how it related to the 1987 storm. The cycle covers a period of approximately 150 years:

The reason it broke through in '87 was it had a wonderful storm to work with, but also because of the tidal dynamics which was changed over the

150-year period. When the inlet is way up north, then Chatham Harbor responds pretty quickly to what the ocean tides are. As the barrier beach grows southward, then the tide takes longer to get into Chatham Harbor from the ocean, and as time goes on, it takes longer and longer, and so finally, in the 1960s, '70s and into the '80s, it got down to Monomoy, so the tides were a really small range inside Chatham Harbor, compared to the ocean. That's a huge differential, so when you get a huge storm, it over washes it, then it's kind of like a waterfall coming down and rushing in, and then an inlet forms, and then there's a big low tide after that, so it rushes out again.

The rest of the Cape was also feeling the storm's impact, particularly in Sandwich. The *Village Broadsider* reported that ten- to fifteen-foot waves rolled in over Salt Marsh Road on the Spring Hill barrier beach: "A seaside mobile hung untouched from the open ceiling. Floor-length drapes swayed gently back and forth in the breeze. The walls, deck and glass that once separated the cottage from the elements were gone. Gone in one of the fiercest storms to hit the Sandwich coast in many years."

Chatham Bar, as shown in 1987, a few months after the northeaster of January 1987 broke through the barrier beach. *NASA.*

Front decks were ripped off and washed away, leaving the main living quarters hanging on the edge of twelve-foot banks. The high tide also flooded the marshes and cottages along North Shore Boulevard, while River Street and Dewey Avenue were closed due to flooding, and state police closed Route 6A after the tide rolled into Scorton Creek and over the bridge. Michael Weldon of North Shore Boulevard saw the tide gushing through a deep crack in his cellar floor. "It's coming in like a river," he told the *Cape Cod Times*. "I can only pray for a miracle that the tide turns around." It didn't. "I've never seen such waves and devastation in my life," fire department lieutenant Brian Gallant said after inspecting damage along Springhill Beach. The storm even hurled a four-hundred-pound hot tub from one home on Springhill Beach to the opposite end of the beach, Gallant said.

At Sandy Neck, a six-mile-long barrier beach in West Barnstable, "a classic northeaster, on the heels of a series of other strong winter storms, joined forces with an unusual planetary alignment to bring some of the highest tides of the century to the mid-Cape," the *Register* noted. Blowouts (breaks in the face of the dune barrier) widened into breakthroughs (a more complete fissure), allowing water through the barrier to travel across the 1,900-foot width of Sandy Neck into the Great Marshes.

In Dennis, the intersection of Dr. Bottero and Chapin Beach Road was completely washed out, cutting off access to Chapin Beach, the *Register* said. Beaches were littered with debris, mostly brush and tree stumps, which had been placed between the dunes between Chapin and Corporation Beaches. This measure was meant to protect the dunes, but the material was just lifted up and scattered along the beaches, doing little to limit erosion. A female white-sided dolphin stranded and died at Sesuit Beach in East Dennis, despite the efforts of a rescue team to push it back to sea. They were unable to load the eight-foot-long mammal onto a truck due to high tides on the beach.

The bottom half of the wooden beach stairway at Marconi Beach in Wellfleet was destroyed. Parts of downtown Provincetown flooded, and four feet of water poured into the Mews Restaurant on Commercial Street. Waves crashed over MacMillan Wharf for the first time since the 1978 blizzard, while nearly a foot and a half of water came into Commercial Street at the Gosnold Street landing.

THE NICKERSON CAMP SURVIVES

Following the storm, the Nickerson Beach Camp on Chatham's outer bar, constructed in 1947, "sat precariously just north of the breach," according to the Chatham Historical Society's Nickerson Beach Camp exhibit at the Atwood House Museum on Stage Harbor Road. Knowing that the structure was living on borrowed time, Joshua A. Nickerson Jr., son of the original owner, donated it to the Chatham Historical Society. In 1990, it was jacked up, put on wheels, rolled along the North Beach flats and then floated on a barge across Chatham Harbor to the grounds of the Atwood House Museum, complete with the interior furnishings, iron wood stove, old-fashioned icebox, soapstone sink with hand pump, kerosene lamps, double bunks and three ship drawings, plus the outhouse. The following year, several North Beach camps would be claimed by the elements. As the Chatham Historical Society noted, "The move was none too soon."

The Nickerson Beach Camp was moved from North Beach to the Chatham Historical Society's Atwood House Museum in 1990. *Author's collection.*

HURRICANE BOB

1991

The seawall at Menahaunt Road consists of about thirty to thirty-five huge blocks of concrete. The surge of Vineyard Sound submerged the entire outboard half of the road, dislodged about twenty-four of those barriers, which [Falmouth Public Works director William] *Owens said weigh fifteen tons each, and scattered them across the road and the front lawns of the houses, as a child would scatter toy building blocks on the living room rug.*
—Falmouth Enterprise, *August 23, 1991*

When hurricanes come calling along the New England coast, they have their origins in one of two places: off the Cape Verde Islands in the eastern Atlantic Ocean or near the Bahamas in the Caribbean Sea. The former can take over a week to arrive on the Eastern Seaboard, while the Bahama storms have been known to roll up the coast in just a few days.

On August 19, 1991, the latter situation was taking place along the Eastern Seaboard. Hurricane Bob was off the coast of Cape Hatteras, making a beeline for the New England coast. By day's end, it would be the most destructive hurricane to hit Cape Cod since the one-two cyclonic punch of Carol and Edna in 1954.

Bob was a weak Category 2 storm by the time it made landfall in Newport, Rhode Island, at about 2:30 p.m. At that point, the system began to expand. "When Bob met the colder waters near the Cape, it lost its eye altogether," Glenn Field, the warning coordination meteorologist for the Boston National Weather Service office in Norton, Massachusetts, noted in a 2023 interview. "It took on almost a winter storm type of appearance." The storm walloped

Cape Cod with 90-mile-per-hour winds, with gusts of 125 miles per hour reported at Woods Hole and Truro. The *Cape Cod Times* reported a storm surge of nine to fifteen feet in Buzzards Bay. Field summed up Bob's visit to Cape Cod this way:

> *Hurricane Bob was nothing more than a cluster of thunderstorms down here* [pointing to the Bahamas] *on a Friday afternoon, not even a tropical depression yet, just a disturbance. Over the weekend, it turned into a major hurricane, then weakened a little as it came up here, but like most New England hurricanes, it was in for breakfast and out for dinner.*

Once again, it was the Buzzards Bay area that felt the worst of the hurricane's wrath. Bob was blamed for three deaths and caused close to $1 billion in damage. According to the *Boston Globe*, Bob barreled up the coast with a forward speed of thirty-five miles per hour, sweeping into Narragansett Bay before crossing over southeastern Massachusetts. The storm damaged or destroyed hundreds of boats, snapped trees and sent some hurtling through houses, smashed windows, ripped the roofs off buildings and triggered tidal surges that caused flooding in oceanfront communities. Fortunately for those on the Cape, Bob arrived during low tide. The *Provincetown Advocate* noted the Outer Cape's good fortune:

> *The tide, which was dead low about 1:30 p.m. and stayed out during the storm, was still ten feet higher than normal due to the hurricane. If the tide had been high, much of Provincetown and Beach Point in Truro might have been wiped off the map by the storm surge, the real killer in hurricanes.*

In Falmouth, the town was coming off a busy weekend with the running of the annual Falmouth Road Race the day before. Conditions began to worsen around midday, but people went on with their usual activities, the *Falmouth Enterprise* reported: "Even as the storm started to hit early Monday afternoon, swimmers were spotted in the churning waters of the sound in Falmouth Heights and others were seen walking or driving along the town's roads while the winds snapped trees like matchsticks."

With wind speeds blowing at eighty miles per hour, the Sagamore and Bourne Bridges were closed at 2:30 p.m. The strongest winds on the Cape were felt between 2:00 and 4:00 p.m.

In Falmouth, Walter McLean and his family hunkered down for the storm and then went out to Surf Drive after the worst of the hurricane was over.

He told the *Cape Cod Times* in 2001 that the water was waist-deep across the road, recently repaved for the Falmouth Road Race. Falmouth Public Works director William Owen told the *Falmouth Enterprise* that Bob "picked up a couple hundred feet of Surf Drive, like someone lifting a pancake with a spatula, and moved it twenty-five feet toward the pond."

The *Enterprise* also told the story of Frank and Alice Hicks of Mashpee, who watched as a fifty-year-old tree came crashing down on their porch and house. Frank Hicks, seventy-four, built the house in 1940. He was able to push the side door open far enough to stick his arm and hand out and pull away an awning that had fallen against the door. The front door was completely blocked by the tree. In New Seabury, the ocean tore a forty-yard gap in Popponessett Spit.

Main Street in Bourne was flooded by water from the Cape Cod Canal and Cohasset Narrows that spilled onto the commercial strip, with water reaching just short of the doors of local businesses, according to the *Bourne Courier*. Three cars were seen floating at Kingman Marine at Red Brook Harbor.

In Barnstable Village, Charles Orloff, the principal of the Mattacheese Middle School in Yarmouth, was driving through when "all of a sudden a

High tides from Hurricane Bob flooded the parking lot outside the Lighthouse Inn. *Lighthouse Inn, West Dennis, Massachusetts.*

wall of wind came in and trees started coming down in front of me." Orloff told the *Cape Cod Times* that debris was pelting the side of his car, and at one point he stopped his car and lay flat on the sidewalk of Route 6A in front of the Barnstable County Courthouse. "Not very smart," admitted Orloff, who has also served as the executive director of the Blue Hill Observatory in Milton, Massachusetts. In the Centerville section of Barnstable, several trees came down around Our Lady of Victory Church, but the church's statue of Mary remained intact, according to the publication *And Bob Was His Name: Hurricane Bob, a Diary of Destruction, August 19, 1991.*

In West Dennis, the Lighthouse Inn was once again doing battle with the elemental fury of the tropics. The lower deck took another wipeout hit, as six feet of water poured in and then out the back doors. According to the historic dateline compiled by the inn, 125 guests and employees were evacuated to Bishop's Terrace in West Harwich, where they sat out the storm, eating lunch and dinner that was prepared without electricity while they witnessed the nearby steeple of the Baptist church blowing out. Members of the Stone family, the inn's owners, and employees remained to move furniture. According to the inn's report, "Bob Stone was caught in the flow of water pouring through the grounds, and he managed to drive his van to the hill by the cottages, where he spent the entire storm watching over the property."

That evening, guests returned to their rooms and cottages, although there was no electricity and the grounds were devastated. They all left the following day. The damage included:

> *Three feet of seaweed plugged the chain link fence around the tanning courts. A striped bass was found in the lower deck, along with jellyfish, crabs, mollusks, and seaweed. Electricity was out for over a week, and the only hot water available was at the pool, so cleanup had to be done with buckets of water hauled from the pool area. Any food that could be saved was sent to Bishop's Terrace, which remained open every night, and had electricity restored in three days. Lighthouse Inn reopened with no access to the Lower Deck on August 29. Over a million dollars of damage occurred.*

Just to the east of West Dennis Beach, which also sustained damage on its roads, controversy had broken out earlier in the month over a chain-link fence that the Town of Dennis had installed across the jetty at the mouth of Swan River. The Massachusetts Department of Environmental Protection had ruled that Dennis officials violated the law with the installation and

The lower level of the Lighthouse Inn sustained heavy damage following another flood, this time from Hurricane Bob. *Lighthouse Inn, West Dennis, Massachusetts.*

offered three options to natural resources officer George Macdonald—file for a license, prove a license wasn't needed or tear down the fence. Before Macdonald could make a decision, the hurricane hit, and the fence disappeared. According to the *Register*, "Hurricane Bob decided the issue for him."

LOWER, OUTER CAPE NOT SPARED

In Harwich, several boats were grounded in Allen and Wychmere Harbors. The *Cape Codder* reported in January 1992 that Harbormaster Tom Leach provided these statistics: Bob sank twenty-three boats and beached and damaged fifty-nine more. "My own boat got Bobbed," he added. Roland and June Gallant of Brewster witnessed the locust trees falling across their doors, temporarily blocking their only exits from the house.

In Orleans, both the Jonathan Young Windmill and the Captain Linnell Restaurant were damaged, according to *And Bob Was His Name*. The exterior

Gail Nickerson, *center*, and her children pose in front of the damaged Jonathan Young Windmill in Orleans after Hurricane Bob. *Gail Nickerson.*

The Odd Fellows Hall in Orleans saw damage to the side of the building during Hurricane Bob. *Gail Nickerson.*

of the Odd Fellows Hall on Namskaket Road sustained damage. Town workers were assisted by fifty Community of Jesus members to do repairs. Souvenirs were available in Orleans too. "For $15, the concessionaire at Nauset Beach will sell you an official Hurricane Bob tie-dyed t-shirt. 'Surf's up,' it says in one corner," the *Cape Codder* reported.

At the tip of the Cape, Truro and Provincetown both saw extensive damage. According to the *Cape Codder*, a Truro woman on Higgins Hollow Road "saw a 100-year-old tree in her yard go straight up in the air, then topple over." The Outermost Reach Motel on Route 6 in North Truro lost the roof of its restaurant, with the walls collapsing on the front side of the building.

In Provincetown, thirty-five boats sank in the harbor and forty-three washed up on the beach, according to the *Provincetown Advocate*. There were two airborne rooftops. The roof of the Sandcastle Resort on Route 6A along the border of the two towns blew off and crushed three cars. Three people were injured by flying debris. "We had a rain shower of shingles…and then the siding started coming off," Kerry Elliott of Ontario, who was staying at the Sandcastle, told the *Cape Codder*. Cathy Elliott added that they "heard the rumble" of the roof, and then she "grabbed the baby and ran for the closet." Cecelia Veara, the front desk clerk at the Sandcastle, told the *Provincetown Advocate* that the entire roof of the building closest to the bay "blew right off its hinges." Yellow insulation blew all over the property and coated the fence of the tennis courts. Debris flying from the roof also tore through power lines that led into town.

The *Cape Codder* also reported that the Surfside Inn on Commercial Street lost its lid; it landed a block away. In a 2023 interview, Linda Ersoy, who was living on Commercial Street at the time (and later became the general manager of the Sandcastle), roamed down her street. She recalled, "There were a lot of people partying in the streets, 'hurricane parties.' There was just a lot of wind, not much rain. I was out there until a roof went flying by, and that's when I went back inside."

According to the *Cape Codder*, the Tides Inn lost part of its roof, while a concrete wall at the Boatslip crumbled. Rick's Restaurant and the Provincetown Inn lost some roofing, while Commercial Street resident Elena Hall lost her entire roof.

Even though it took nearly a week to restore power in Provincetown, it was still Carnival Week. The *Cape Codder* noted that a benefit performance of *Vampire Lesbians of Sodom* went on by candlelight at the Gifford House.

This page: The roof of Sandcastle Resort on Route 6A in Provincetown was torn off by Hurricane Bob's wind gusts. *Sandcastle Resort, Provincetown, Massachusetts.*

As Bob exited the Cape region, passing to the east of Boston, normal life began to resume, very slowly. Page one of the next day's *Cape Codder* newspaper summed it up this way:

> *Hurricane Bob was a feast for the senses late Monday when people began to emerge from their houses. The air was filled with the scent of pine and oak from the many shorn and uprooted trees. Area waters were whipped into a mass of frothy white foam and mist, and the sound of massive gusts howling through telephone wires was eerie. Even the feel of the atmosphere as the barometer plunged was unique.*

On Fowler Lane in Falmouth, a "mini-diary" of the event, in the form of handwritten signs, was posted along the road. According to the photograph by the *Boston Herald's* Ted Fitzgerald, these were some of the highlights:

> *Hurricane Bob Running Events*
> *12:00–1:00—Water, waves cross Surf Dr.; Water Around Yellow House on Mill Road.*
> *1:00–2:00—Pond Overflow Enters Salt Pond Road and Fowlers Lane; Houses from Surf Drive Afloat in Pond.*
> *2:00–3:00—Houses from Surf Drive Land Across Pond; Water Is Through All Little Cottages on Left Mill Rd.; Water Is at These Hedges.*
> *4:00–5:00—Water and Wind Starts to Abate.*
> *Feelings: "Excited," "Dead," "Sad," "Grateful," "Friendship," "Lucky—Alive!," among others.*

For the next few weeks, summer life resumed. Angry yellow jackets, their nests disrupted by the storm, went on a stinging rampage across the Cape, according to the *Times*. As the year advanced into autumn, it would be all too clear that Mother Nature wasn't done with Cape Cod.

THE NO-NAME/HALLOWEEN/
PERFECT STORM

1991

Although [the National Hurricane Center] *considered classifying this as a hurricane,* [the National Meteorological Center], *NHC, and* [National Weather Service] *Headquarters decided against this to avoid unnecessarily confusing and alarming the public.*
—"*Natural Disaster Survey Report: The Halloween Nor'easter,*" *NOAA, 1992*

Bruce and Donna Edson experienced their share of storms while staying at their beach camp in the "Second Village" of North Beach in Chatham over the years, but they began thinking something wasn't quite right in the days leading up to Halloween 1991. Stormy weather had begun to settle in over the last couple of days, and even the waves on the usually tranquil bay were breaking to heights of five feet.

By the morning of October 29, the Edsons knew this wasn't going to be any ordinary storm. In fact, it would end up being labeled as "Perfect" in the history books. This wild weather system, labeled as the "No-Name Storm," the "Halloween Northeaster" and finally the "Perfect Storm," belted the Cape for four days with winds that topped out at seventy-nine miles per hour. A weather buoy off Nova Scotia recorded a wave exceeding one hundred feet, while east of the Cape, buoys measured wave heights at thirty-nine feet. A continuous high tide swept away seventeen of the rustic beach camps on North Beach.

The Edsons "were marooned," Donna Edson told the *Register* newspaper later that week, but thanks to several neighbors and friends who staged what she called "a heroic rescue" by ORVs, they were taken ashore. "We were very lucky," she said.

Greeted by a flooded driveway in the morning hours, the Edsons and their beach neighbor, Patrick O'Connell of the camp known as the Nauset Hilton, took to a high dune to watch the surf. While their camps were safe, two others—the Hallock and Lund camps—were not. According to Bruce Edson's account in Frances L. Higgins's book *Drifting Memories: The Nauset Beach Camps on Cape Cod*, one wave came in and took out the wall of the Hallock camp, followed by two more that swept it away. When Donna Edson couldn't see the Lund camp, "they got edgy," the *Register* reported. Adding to their distress was the fact that their vehicles were partially submerged. Bruce then alerted the Coast Guard. "They [the Edsons] wanted off big time," Chatham police chief Barry Eldredge said.

Police and Coast Guard officials were planning to hoist them out of the predicament by helicopter or by inflatable vessel across the harbor, but time was of the essence. Enter Bill Hammatt, Lynn and Nelson Long, Rob Angell and some other friends who convoyed out in four-wheel-drive vehicles. Deputy police chief Wayne Love accompanied the group as far as he could but decided not to risk going any farther. Hammatt gave this account of the ride to the *Register*: "It was the worst ride down and back I've ever had, and I've been driving it for a few years. Waves crashed over each vehicle and it appeared a few times that the rescue effort could not go forward."

Finally, one of the ORVs got close enough to the Edson camp. According to *Drifting Memories*, the Edsons; their poodle, Jingles; and O'Connell had to wade through chest-deep water. Into the vehicles they all went, but this wasn't going to be any ordinary ride back to civilization. Angell provided these details for *Drifting Memories*: "The ride off the beach was pedal to the metal. Your foot is stuck right to the floor, and the transmissions are heating up. The sand is nothing but soup, and you're sinking in. So if you stop you're going to get stuck. The adrenaline is pumping."

Hammatt and the Longs lost their own camps. The roof of Hammatt's camp ended up at the Cow Yard, with his refrigerator wedged in too. "Inside, an egg had somehow survived the journey intact," the *Cape Cod Times* noted. Angell's camp was picked up by the ocean on Wednesday night and deposited about two thousand feet south of its original location. "Although the house had moved, decorative glass bottles stayed on their shelves inside the camp, unmoved and undamaged," the *Times* said. The rest of the building was a total loss. For Robert Crowell of Dennis, all that remained of his North Beach camp was a bent-over flagpole.

Unlike many beach camp owners, Colin Fuller turned the storm into money in the bank. About a year before the storm, he had purchased the former Starkweather camp from Peter Collingworth, who had drawn up plans to move the building. The storm then buried the camp. According to *Drifting Memories*, this led to the construction of the new Fuller-Coppedge Camp nearby: "For us this was the Perfect Storm. Not only did I not have to pay to get somebody to move the camp, but also then I got the insurance from it to build this place. I rebuilt in 1992."

By 2008, the ocean was closing in on the cottage. Surf was coming in through the windows, according to the *Provincetown Banner*. Mike Winkler of Truro and his crane company were hired to move it. As Winkler recalled in a 2016 interview, "We were hired to take down five beach camps in Chatham, and took most of them off the beach in dumpsters. This cottage was lying in the surf. It was probably one tide away from being washed away. It had a massive hole in it and was full of sand and water was lapping through."

Winkler had it put on a barge and towed to Ryder's Cove, where it sat while owners Fuller and Copey Coppedge tried to have it repaired. After several options were weighed, they sold it to Winkler, who developed a fondness for the cottage, for one dollar. Winkler then had the sixteen-by-thirty-two-foot cottage moved to Provincetown Harbor, where, as of 2023, he was using it as a "staycation" houseboat.

Across the harbor from North Beach, high surf destroyed the forty-foot bank supporting the scenic overlook at Lighthouse Beach. Homes along the shore from the Fish Pier to Morris Island sustained heavy damage. When the storm finally burned itself out on November 1, Chatham emerged to examine what nature had left behind, according to the *Cape Codder*: "Meteorologist John LaCorte said his colleagues at the [National Weather Service] station on Morris Island in Chatham called the storm 'the worst they've ever seen.' The opinion was seconded by many people out and about on Wednesday, surveying damage."

A Storm for the Ages

First dubbed the "Halloween Nor'easter" by the National Weather Service, the storm was an unusual combination of three weather systems—a powerful low-pressure area, a strong cold front and the fading elements of Hurricane

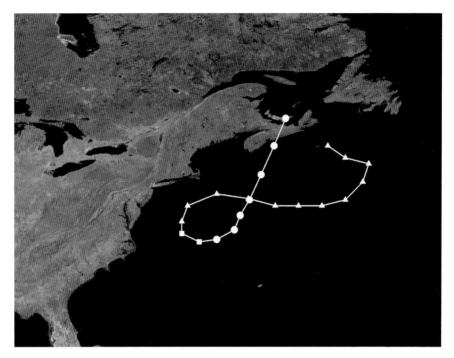

The "No-Name Storm," also known as the "Halloween Gale" and the "Perfect Storm," twisted and turned in the North Atlantic Ocean before making landfall in Canada. *NOAA*.

Grace. While the storm's wrath was strongest along the Massachusetts coast, its impact was felt from Newfoundland to Puerto Rico.

The National Park Service, in a "Storms of Record" article for its website, quoted meteorologist Stu Ostro of the Weather Channel, who called the system "an extraordinary confluence of atmospheric ingredients" and "unique in its evolution." Ostro then found it difficult to categorize the storm:

> *A non-tropical system absorbing a tropical one is not unprecedented, nor is a tropical cyclone developing from a non-tropical system. But for both processes to occur with the same system, not to mention one of this magnitude, is what made the cyclone so amazing. To me, this was the ultimate "hybrid" storm.*

The system lashed most of eastern New England, claiming thirteen lives, and was front and center in Sebastian Junger's book *The Perfect Storm*, a title that was coined from a conversation between Junger, a summer resident of Truro, and Boston National Weather Service forecaster Robert Case.

The U.S. Coast Guard cutter *Tamaroa* rescued three people from the sailboat *Satori* during the "No-Name Storm." *U.S. Coast Guard.*

Junger's book focused on the loss of the Gloucester fishing boat *Andrea Gail*, as well as the rescue of the three-person crew of the thirty-two-foot sailboat *Satori* by the U.S. Coast Guard cutter *Tamaroa*. "I thought I was going to die," Karen Stimpson told the *Cape Cod Times* of their ordeal, which occurred about 120 miles south of Nantucket. After unsuccessful rescue attempts by boat, a helicopter from Air Station Cape Cod hoisted Karen and two other crew members from the *Satori*. The *Times* added that five minutes after they were brought in, another helicopter brought in the five-member crew of the fishing vessel *Michelle Lane*, which ran aground off Noman's Land, a tiny island just south of Martha's Vineyard.

CHAOS ACROSS THE CAPE

Back on land, the rising seas were causing havoc from one end of the Cape to the other. "Cape Cod is smaller today than it was just a few days ago," the

Cape Codder said, but it could have been substantially worse, David Aubrey, director of the Coastal Research Center at the Woods Hole Oceanographic Institution, told the *Cape Cod Times*. Aubrey said that the region was fortunate to be in a "neap tidal period," which occurs between the first and third quarters of the lunar month. It's the period of the smallest tidal phase, when there is the least difference between high and low tides: "The highest tide now is about a foot lower than it was last week at this time, or than it will be next week at this time. If the storm had occurred a week later or earlier, there would have been more damage because the highest tides would have been higher."

In its 1992 National Disaster Survey Report, the National Oceanic and Atmospheric Administration (NOAA) noted that tides were three to four feet above the normal high tide along the entire Massachusetts coast.

At Ballston Beach in Truro, those tides broke through to the freshwater Pamet River, leaving an eighty-two-foot cut through the dunes. "I never thought I'd see it in my life," Provincetown native Edward Roza told the *Cape Codder*. Nancy Dingman Watson, who lived several hundred yards from the beach, told the *Times* that there was nearly two feet of water in the beach parking lot, and seawater foam was at her door.

John Moore Jr. of Kingston, Pennsylvania, and friend Barbara Musnuff were asleep in his Ballston Beach home during the worst of the storm. They didn't know about the break until the next morning. "The windows were covered with seaweed and foam so we could not see out," Musnuff said. "It was like watching a science fiction movie." Two to three feet of foam surrounded the house after the storm, according to the *Cape Codder*.

Five feet of water poured into the basement of the Mews Restaurant in Provincetown, with the water level reaching into the main electrical panel and shorting it out, the *Provincetown Advocate* reported. Two boats washed over the West End breakwater, while the schooner *Hindu* rammed into the Coast Guard pier, damaging both boat and pier. Portions of Commercial Street were flooded on both ends of town, and the Provincetown Inn rotary was under water.

Along the outer beach, tides washed back twelve feet of embankment to the parking lot at Newcomb Hollow Beach in Wellfleet, the *Advocate* reported, while the *Cape Cod Times* noted the stairway at Marconi Beach in Wellfleet was a tidal victim. The ocean chopped away forty to fifty feet of sand from the Nauset Beach dunes in Orleans, while four to five feet of erosion left the northern end of Nauset Beach Light Road "dangerously close to the edge," the *Times* reported.

At Eastham's Coast Guard Beach, Nauset Spit experienced several wash-overs, and the high coastal bank north of the Coast Guard station was knocked flat. The access bridge, constructed after the 1978 storm, was damaged. An eleven-thousand-year-old Indian campsite, discovered after a November 1990 storm, found itself in harm's way. Prior to the storm, a large dune had protected the archaeological site, the *Boston Globe* reported. The boathouse owned by Eastham's Henry McCusker was swept into Nauset Marsh, with the entire roof washing ashore near Hemenway Landing.

Route 28 in Harwich in the area near Pleasant Bay was under water. In the middle of the flooded area, reported the *Cape Codder*, "was a man perched atop his car, which was sitting like a tin island in the middle of Route 28."

On the Upper Cape, Popponesset Spit in Mashpee and Surf Drive in Falmouth, both hit hard by Hurricane Bob two months earlier, sustained further damage. On Salt Marsh Road in Sandwich, several homes were damaged, the *Cape Cod Times* said. Pipes pushed up from the sand and stairs leading nowhere was all that was left of the house at 82 Salt Marsh Road. Pieces and planks from the boardwalk along Town Beach, still recovering from Hurricane Bob, ended up on Dewey Avenue. In Yarmouth Port, the one-thousand-foot boardwalk at Gray's Beach was completely destroyed.

At Town Cove in Orleans, two feet of water made its way into the Orleans Yacht Club, with more than thirty boats driven into the nearby marsh. "Sand, mud, and seagrass…was just throughout the place," the *Cape Codder* noted, while also making this observation: "When people gather in the decades to come in the Orleans Yacht Club to spin yarns, they'll certainly remember the day the doors were blown off the building, and the water rushed in, and the leather chairs were put on top of tables."

During the years since the Blizzard of '78, Cape Cod beaches had begun to see some sand recovery, but the No-Name Storm proved to be a tremendous setback. In late October, Nat and Mildred Champlin had left their Mission Bell dune shack in Provincetown, only to return on November 1 to evaluate "the damage inflicted by the worst storm we had ever endured." In a 2023 correspondence, Mildred Champlin said that their house had gone through five days of ten high moon tides. She described the scene they witnessed upon their arrival:

> *Clambering out of the car and racing to the dune's edge, we were stunned to be looking down, rather than out over the 100 feet of grass we had a week ago. The storm had clawed away maybe 75 feet of our frontage. The ocean*

This page: The Champlin family returned to Cape Cod after the "No-Name Storm" to find nearly seventy-five feet of sand swept away from the front of their Provincetown dune shack, Mission Bell. *Mildred Champlin.*

was lapping almost at our feet. The dune to the east was demolished and the yard was pock-marked with holes dug by little downdraft whirlwinds. A waste pipe that had been under the sand was exposed and it was easier to duck under it than climb over.

Champlin also expressed gratitude for nearly five decades of life on the dunes: "We viewed the devastation and I said I'd never again look forward predicting the future. All we know is that Mother Nature is in charge and we have to be grateful for all the years we've had and enjoy right now. So far we've been lucky. Another 'Perfect Storm' will come in the future. We know that."

TWENTIETH-CENTURY
NOTABLES AND NEAR-MISSES

As the twentieth century dawned across Cape Cod, the region was still reeling from the destructive impact left by the storm of November 26 and 27, 1898, otherwise known as the *"Portland* Gale." This killer system would go on to be the benchmark of Cape storms, the one all future northeasters and hurricanes would be compared to.

The hurricanes of 1938, 1944, 1954 and 1991, along with the northeasters of 1978 and 1987 and the No-Name storm, all ended up on that elite list of Cape Cod weather events to be remembered. To this day, they're remembered by media outlets and mariners alike on their anniversaries. Over the course of the century, many other weather systems also left their calling cards on the Cape. Some were remembered well; others, particularly those before the 1938 hurricane, have only a few details. Here's a look back at some of the notables and near-misses.

"MARCONI" STORM OF 1901

Newspapers referred to this storm as "the severest gale since 1898," but the highlight of the gale of November 25, 1901, proved to be a bump in the road for wireless telegraph innovator Guglielmo Marconi at his South Wellfleet site.

Marconi, whose wireless stations were linked across the Atlantic, had completed construction of twenty towers on the Outer Cape bluff in 1901. They stood until the storm of November 25, when sixty-mile-per-hour winds lashed the Cape, but it wasn't like Marconi hadn't been warned, wrote Cape Cod National Seashore historian Michael E. Whatley in the 1987 booklet *Marconi Wireless on Cape Cod: South Wellfleet, Massachusetts, 1901–1917*. Many locals were on hand when the towers were built:

> *After construction of his towers in Polhu, England, Guglielmo Marconi set his sights on doing the same in South Wellfleet. The construction project in 1901 drew many locals to the scene.*
>
> *They were fascinated by the project, but like true Cape Codders, were very skeptical of the outcome. Many predicted that the circular arrangement of masts would* [be] *blown down in the next northeast storm, as one mast would pull down the next and so forth and so on.*

"Every single pole was blown down and the houses were partly destroyed," the *Yarmouth Register* said. All twenty towers were knocked over or bent but were quickly replaced with V-shaped antenna suspended between masts. His dreams for a transatlantic wireless connection went on as planned, culminating with the messages between President Theodore Roosevelt and King Edward of England on January 18, 1903.

THE CYCLONE OF JUNE 1904

It only lasted ten minutes or so, according to the *Yarmouth Register* of June 25, 1904, but this "freak of a storm" took down hundreds of trees and damaged many houses across the Cape, particularly in Yarmouth. "The path of the cyclone was in a southwesterly direction through the center of town," the *Register* reported. The paper provided details of one severe incident:

> *A curious freak of a storm was the lifting of the roof of Charles Keene's barn on State Street, which was carried over two houses and landed with terrific force on the rear of the house of John Maley. The rear of Mr. Maley's house was badly damaged but fortunately no one was injured.*

Outside of Yarmouth, wind damage was less, although a man driving through the woods on Forestdale Road in Sandwich went for a ride he didn't bargain for. The wind "lifted the carriage from the center of the road to the gutter, some four or five feet distant," the *Register* said. A severe hailstorm was reported in Sagamore. Lightning was vivid, and heavy rain fell, flooding streets.

THE GREAT GALE OF 1917

The National Oceanic and Atmospheric Administration reports that information concerning the gale of 1917 is "extremely meager," but the storm is known to have claimed dozens of lives at sea. It also appears to have been the force behind the destruction of a windmill along the West Harwich/Dennis Port border.

NOAA has determined that the system was a tropical storm that passed just to the east of Cape Cod on August 10, 1917. Its sudden arrival in the morning hours caught the crews of the schooners *Mary C. Santos* and *Natalie J. Nelson* completely off guard, with nineteen Provincetown fishermen lost between the two vessels.

The *Yarmouth Register* reported that wind gusts peaked at ninety miles per hour, and wave heights were estimated at fifty feet. The *Santos* was about sixty-five miles south-southeast of Highland Light in Truro, with its dories having been over the side for about an hour. The wind quickly picked up out of the southeast and then quickly turned to the northwest. All but two of the dories "were gone from the moment it struck them," the *Register* said. "Struggling men and dead bodies littered the water." The rest of the *Santos* crew was unable to assist in a rescue.

Meanwhile, the *Natalie J. Nelson* was about forty-seven miles south-southeast of Highland Light. Its dories stayed afloat longer than the men of the *Santos* and were picked up before the wind shifted. Twelve men were rescued, but six were lost.

Captain Louis Soars of Provincetown, commander of the schooner *Anna*, was rescued by a crew member after a wave took him over the side. The schooner *Virginia* was swordfishing nearby the *Anna* and witnessed the rescue, but they also spotted the small fishing boats *Stetson* and *Daniel* battling the waves. As the storm pulled away, wreckage could be seen floating around, confirming that the two boats were lost. The sloop *Magnolia* managed to arrive safely in Provincetown but not before sustaining heavy damage. Two of the *Magnolia*'s men were washed overboard and in the water for twenty minutes before they were rescued. "The hardy fishermen's worst danger is from the tornado-like gale," the *Register* said. "This one of Friday morning was typical."

On Division Street, which runs along the border of West Harwich and Dennis Port, a windmill was heavily damaged by the "Great Gale of 1917," according to Gail Nickerson. A photograph, labeled by her husband, Vernon Nickerson, shows Vernon's grandmother as a young woman and "shingles ripped off, no sails and debris on the ground," she said, adding that the damaged windmill was later burned down by local boys.

THE HURRICANE OF 1924

"A severe storm that seemed, indeed, like a tropical hurricane, characteristic of Southern seas," powered its way just to the east of Cape Cod on August 24, 1924. The *Falmouth Enterprise* referred to the Category 1 storm as "one of the most violent summer storms in the history of the Weather Bureau," with seventy-five-mile-per-hour winds and heavy rain that "made the day one of the most disagreeable of the year."

The whaling ship *Wanderer* was wrecked on the rocks off Cuttyhunk Island after the storm drove the bark across Buzzards Bay. The crew, seeing that the vessel was doomed, abandoned ship and set out in boats before landing on Cuttyhunk Island, according to the Mattapoisett Museum's spring 2013 issue of *The Crow's Nest*. Eight men landed on the east side of the island and were rescued by island residents, while seven others made it to the west side of the island before being hauled in by the lightship *Handkerchief* off Sow and Pigs Ledge. The *Wanderer*, which had just been outfitted for whaling and was towed to the entrance of New Bedford Harbor, was the last whaler to leave an American port. It was the bark used in the 1921 film *Down to the Sea in Ships*.

The Cape's oldest windmill, located in West Yarmouth, lost its arms in the storm, the *Barnstable Patriot* noted. Tree damage was extensive, particularly in South Yarmouth and Falmouth. Many elms, maples and fruit trees were taken down in the storm. Damage to fruit and other crops was significant—"the unripe fruit was shaken off, causing a big loss to the growers," the *Enterprise* said. "The Portuguese in the eastern part of [Falmouth] were heavy losers in this respect." In Yarmouth, residents picked their way through debris until darkness fell that night.

The roof of a barn in Teaticket was torn off by the wind, while a falling tree damaged part of the roof of the former Antlers Inn in East Falmouth. The kitchen chimney at the Falmouth Arms crashed through the roof of the hotel. Many boats at Quissett and Woods Hole Harbors were damaged.

Trees blocked several roads in Barnstable, causing traffic standstills. "A typical illustration is that of one party going from Hyannis to a point just beyond Osterville and being obliged to make seven detours," the *Barnstable Patriot* reported.

Gordon Spence recalled his experience in the storm for the *Cape Cod Times* in 1990. Spence and his family were at their cabin in Wellfleet, an experience that he said "was nerve-racking for my parents but very exciting for us children." He told a story of how his brother, John, went to fetch some quahogs from the family "cache" outside, but upon his return, his legs had been sandblasted from the high winds on the beach. Spence noted that the wind at Highland Light in nearby Truro was measured at ninety miles per hour. He said that boats were being blown across Chipman's Cove and deposited high on the shore.

During the storm, friends of the family were camping in tents at the beach. The wind blew their tents down, exposing them and their gear to the raging elements. They loaded what they could into their Model T Fords and started to head to their home off Cape. They bought two axes and used them to chop their way down the highway through fallen trees. It took them nearly all day to get to the canal.

The Northeaster of February 1927

One of the most thorough weather reports provided for the northeaster of February 19–20, 1927, was provided in the pages of Henry Beston's 1928 book, *The Outermost House*. The storm belted the Outer Cape with seventy- to eighty-mile-per-hour winds, and "more sleet had fallen in this storm than the Cape had seen in a generation," Beston wrote. He added that many Cape Codders referred to this storm as "the worst gale known on the Outer Cape since the *Portland* went down with all hands on that terrible November night in '98."

Beston's beach house was located on a dune top along the barrier beach two miles south of the Nauset Coast Guard station in Eastham. Two onslaughts of high surf broke through the barrier beach, leaving his house "no longer looking down upon the sea, but directly into it and just over it." To the north, the surf broke free the skeleton of an ancient wreck from the dune and washed to the south. He described the tidal surge as follows:

> It had crossed the beach, climbed the five-foot wall of the dune levels that run between the great mounds, and was hurling wreckage fifty and sixty feet into the starved white beach grass; the marsh was an immense flooded bay, and the "cuts" between the dunes and the marsh rivers of breakers.

Beston was informed of the plight of the *CG-238*, a seventy-five-foot Coast Guard cutter experiencing engine trouble off Highland Light, by the Coast Guard surfmen of the Nauset station. Two destroyers were sent from Boston to attempt a rescue but could not overcome the elements. The nine-man crew of the *CG-238*, which was on a Prohibition-era "rum patrol" off Cape Cod, was lost when "one mighty engulfing wave swept the boat to destruction," according to the *Boston Globe*.

January 1931 Northeaster

The "near hurricane blow," as the early January storm of 1931 was described by the *Provincetown Advocate*, is perhaps best known for driving the longtime summer residence of playwright Eugene O'Neill into the Atlantic.

The former Peaked Hill Life-Saving Station, owned by O'Neill since 1917 before ownership was transferred to his son the previous summer, was losing ground to the sea for the previous year. Two months prior, a storm had left the building's porch suspended over the water, according to the *Barnstable Patriot*.

O'Neill turned the former lifesaving station into a writing studio, where, according to the *Advocate*, he wrote the *S.S. Glencairn*, *The Hairy Ape* and the preliminary draft of *Anna Christie*.

Waves were so high in Provincetown that they floated the wreck of the schooner *Nancy*, which had wrecked up on the beach five years earlier, farther up the beach, the *Patriot* reported. In Hyannis, the town park was flooded. High tides swept across the end of the old railroad wharf, flooded the lower end of Ocean Street and reached the doors of several summer cottages on the waterfront.

The former Peaked Hill Lifesaving Station, once owned by playwright Eugene O'Neill, fell off the Provincetown dunes into the Atlantic Ocean in January 1931. *Cape Cod National Seashore.*

High tides also swept over Chatham Bar, with water levels so high "that in returning to the ocean it passed up the usual Chatham channel and went over a barrier beach," according to the *Patriot.* In the Pleasant Bay section of Chatham, the Coast Guard halfway house between the Chatham and Old Harbor stations was swept away, as was part of the bluff at Chatham Light.

THE NORTHEASTER OF 1933

In late January 1933, a severe northeaster struck, bringing tides that widened Scorton River in Sandwich by one hundred feet at the harbor. The high tides also cut off land access to the Coast Guard station at the Cape Cod Canal. "The high tide crept around the driveway and visitors and Coast Guardsmen going to the station had to take a dory from the old garage going across the short distance to the station steps," the *Cape Cod News* reported. Two cottages at Spring Hill were ruined when the storm "swept in their front doors, taking furniture and toppling buildings forward."

1936 HURRICANE

Weather forecasters were extremely concerned about a system moving along the Eastern Seaboard during mid-September 1936, but the big blow didn't pan out as they expected. "Not in many years has a weather disturbance been so fully heralded in advance," the *Barnstable Patriot* said. "When it finally arrived—a bit overdue, it must be remarked—it was almost disappointing."

The hurricane, which swiped the Cape with fifty-five-mile-per-hour winds and four inches of rain in Hyannis, took down several power lines yet spared larger substations, transformers and high-tension lines. A $6,000 cabin cruiser went adrift from Barnstable and sank in Wellfleet Harbor. Cape trains were held up by a washout along the canal near Sagamore.

In Chatham, a downed elm tree blocked Main Street traffic. The *Harwich Independent* reported that several boats from Stage Harbor were carried out to sea, and Rock Harbor in Orleans saw substantial damage to fishing and sailing craft. Nauset Beach in Orleans and Chatham, as well as Sandy Neck in Barnstable, was lined with people watching the stormy surf.

HURRICANE DOG (1950)

This storm was the strongest of the 1950 hurricane season, passing nearly one hundred miles east of Cape Cod on September 11, 1950. The impact was still felt on the Cape, as the *Cape Codder* dubbed it "the biggest storm since the 1944 hurricane." The paper also added that "the storm did damage, but there was no general havoc." Wind gusts topped out at eighty-one miles per hour at Otis Air Base, the *Falmouth Enterprise* said.

A seventy-mile-per-hour wind gust bowled over a vehicle driven by Christopher Tracy, age twenty, in South Wellfleet. He died at Cape Cod Hospital in Hyannis. At Otis, Staff Sargent Lesley Gott was "temporarily paralyzed" when he came in contact with electric power on Main Street in Falmouth, according to reports in the *Cape Codder* and the *Enterprise*. He was taken to the station hospital and recovered quickly.

At sea, where conditions were at their worst, the *Eugenia J.* of New Bedford, a forty-eight-foot swordfishing boat, was caught off Highland Light and barely made it to Provincetown Harbor, the *Cape Codder* reported. Waves broke over the craft several times, leaving the captain, Myron Parsons of

Malden, waist deep in water. He called it the worst storm in fifty years. A big party boat, the *Katherine II*, was smashed to bits against the West End breakwater in Provincetown.

In Chatham, the large window of the First National store was blown out, according to the *Cape Codder*. In Orleans, storm winds mangled the new Reno Diner neon sign, the *Central Cape Press* said.

The outer beach area of Orleans was filled with people who were "amazed at the sight of breakers estimated to be thirty feet in height," the *Central Cape Press* said. Two piers—the Orleans Town Wharf pier and the Orleans Yacht Club—were severely damaged. The Orleans Yacht Club became a "veritable island," according to the *Press*, as the record high tide encircled the yacht club building.

The 1950 hurricane season was the first of three years when Atlantic hurricanes were named using the Joint Army/Navy Phonetic Alphabet.

THE *PENDLETON* BLIZZARD OF 1952

The raging blizzard of February 18, 1952, is best known for the daring rescue of thirty-two men from the 534-foot tanker *Pendleton* by Bernie Webber and the Coast Guard crew of the *CG-36500* off Chatham's shore. As the *Cape Codder* said, the Coast Guard "staged one of the most brilliant rescue operations in its history off the treacherous Chatham Bars in the teeth of the winter's worst blizzard." Webber and his crew somehow made it to the tanker while navigating through thirty-five-foot waves and blinding snow and sleet.

The storm was also the likely culprit behind the fire that destroyed the Snow Library in Orleans that night. The storm started as an ice storm and took town high-tension lines. Leo Cummings of the volunteer fire department theorized that the lines must have hit the library and started the fire, the *Cape Codder* said.

Lost in the fire was a parchment copy of the Act of Incorporation of the Town of Orleans, signed by President John Adams, and an old slate tombstone of the Reverend Samuel Treat, the third pastor of Eastham's first church.

HURRICANES CONNIE AND DIANE (1955)

During the week of August 8 to 12, 1955, Hurricane Connie was considered to be a dire threat to the Upper Cape region. This led to "an off-Cape stampede of vacation visitors," according to the *Falmouth Enterprise*. Early on Saturday, August 13, the Boston Weather Bureau issued a warning that the Cape would be hit, but at 3:30 a.m., the advisory was changed. The storm would pass the area, with only an occasional blustery squall, but the message reached Falmouth late. "The fire whistles blew the seven-blast hurricane warning," the *Enterprise* said.

Within the week, Connie would be followed by Hurricane Diane, which weakened to a tropical storm by the time it reached New England. According to Glenn Field of the National Weather Service's Boston office in Norton, Massachusetts, in a 2023 interview, "the rainy side of Diane came along the southern New England coast. Five to six inches of rain fell in the Provincetown area."

HURRICANE DONNA (1960)

"Hurricane Donna was a mean gal," the *Barnstable Patriot* proclaimed in its September 15, 1960 edition. Indeed it was, even though the storm "deviated but not too far from the path predicted by the Weather Bureau," according to the *Cape Cod Times*. Donna made its first landfall on Long Island and then over Bridgeport, Connecticut, where it then tracked inland over Central Massachusetts. Donna hit to the west of Block Island instead of east, as was predicted. The Cape still felt wind gusts of ninety miles per hour. The *Falmouth Enterprise* noted that tides were three to four feet above normal.

Dennis was hit particularly hard, with the Lighthouse Inn taking yet another cyclonic hit. According to the inn's historic dateline, the Pavilion went down during the storm for the fourth time, and this time it was not rebuilt. Damage was done to the grounds and lower deck. The wooden floor downstairs was pushed up with sand, destroying the wooden encasings around the steel girders. Employees and family members were rescued by Chatham Coast Guard DUKW boats.

The *Dennis-Yarmouth Register* reported cars flocked to both entrances of West Dennis Beach to see the surf crash over the sea wall and against the Lighthouse Inn. Lower County Road was swamped out in three places, and

A combination of photographs from the Lighthouse Inn shows the damage done by Hurricane Donna in 1960. *Lighthouse Inn, West Dennis, Massachusetts.*

the road along West Dennis Beach going to the jetty was wrecked for about a half mile. People were standing on the Bass River Bridge watching logs, rafts and stray boats float by. The *Register* featured a front-page photograph of a damaged seaside cottage called, appropriately enough, "Storm Tossed."

The West Yarmouth Drive-In screen, "guaranteed to withstand 130 mile-per-hour winds," according to the *Register*, cracked. In Yarmouth Port, a long line of cars waited for highway crews to remove a fallen tree from the road so they could continue sightseeing. In Provincetown, light poles at MacMillan Pier were bent over, according to the *Provincetown Advocate.*

The fifty-foot steel weather tower at Nobska Light in Falmouth was blown over, according to the *Falmouth Enterprise.* Falmouth reported a low barometric pressure of twenty-nine inches.

Dr. Oscar Tenenbaum of the Boston Weather Bureau told the *Cape Cod Times* that hurricane preparedness conferences held in New Bedford, Hyannis and Providence, Rhode Island, over the summer helped keep the hurricane's toll to a minimum. "The record speaks for itself," he said. "People took the situation more calmly."

THE KENNEDY INAUGURAL STORM OF 1961

This blizzard rolled its way over the Eastern Seaboard from January 19 to 21, 1961, just as John F. Kennedy was being sworn in as president of the United States. It also left its calling card on Kennedy's beloved Cape Cod.

Nearly a foot of snow fell, winds gusted to sixty miles per hour and temperatures ranged from six above to twelve below zero. Exceptionally high tides occurred at the same time. Along the Cape's outer beaches, which were only seven months away from being included in the Cape Cod National Seashore, many of the smaller beach camps took a hit.

On Nauset Beach in Orleans, the former Harold Seavey cottage was lifted from its foundation and moved thirty feet across the sand, the *Cape Codder* reported. Farther down the beach in Chatham, the E. Calreton Small beach cottage was destroyed. Joseph A. Nickerson of North Chatham was watching the beach through binoculars and at 5:00 p.m. on Friday called the Smalls to tell them that their cottage had disappeared. Not until Sunday were the Smalls able to go down to the beach by Jeep to see what had happened. As they passed the Seavey cottage, they stopped to look in a window. "It's hard to believe, but a bottle of aspirin was still standing upright on a kitchen shelf," the Smalls said.

At the site of their cottage, they first found their studio couch and then, farther down the beach, only the roof of the cottage. Under the roof were mattresses and a tablecloth; nearby was a gas range.

The high tides flooded across highways in Brewster at Betty's Curve and also in Dennis and Wellfleet, causing police to close them temporarily. The Bernard Collins home on Town Cove in Eastham had thirty-two inches of water in the cellar.

HURRICANE ESTHER (1961)

Hurricane Esther, the first large tropical cyclone to be discovered by satellite imagery, came up the coast from the Caribbean, with the Cape bracing for a major blow. However, just south of the Cape, Esther encountered cooler water, dropping it to tropical storm status. The storm then circled just south of the region before making landfall on the Cape as a tropical storm, according to the National Weather Service.

Esther packed a storm surge of four to six feet, with peak wind gusts of ninety-seven miles per hour at the *Nantucket* lightship and seventy miles per hour at Chatham. The *Falmouth Enterprise* said that its hometown had a daylong northeaster with sixty- to seventy-mile-per-hour winds and two and a half inches of rain.

THE NORTHEASTER OF JANUARY 1966

Provincetown draggers referred to the storm of January 22–23, 1966, as the worst "since the 1938 hurricane," according to the *Provincetown Advocate*. Wind gusts reached one hundred miles per hour at Eastham and seventy-five miles per hour at Provincetown. Four vessels went adrift in Provincetown Harbor and needed the Coast Guard to come to their rescue.

The *Silver Mink*, which was docked at MacMillan Wharf, suffered $4,000 in damage, but it could have been closer to $25,000 had it not been for the Coast Guard's assistance. The *Silver Mink* had its three-thousand-pound power boom torn off, and Captain Manuel Phillips was taken to his vessel by the Coast Guard, who assisted him in what he called "a nightmare of an experience. Everything on board was swinging!" "Everything that could come loose" was in the clutch of the wind, as the men tried to get "everything fastened down," the captain said.

The *Dorchester*, a 107-foot fishing boat out of Portland, Maine, carrying twenty thousand pounds of fish, was about thirty miles off Nauset Light in Eastham when its wires become tangled in its propeller and it became unable to navigate, the *Advocate* reported. Battling the high winds, the *Dorchester* sent out an SOS call to the Coast Guard in Boston, which dispatched the cutter *Cape George* out of Woods Hole. The *Dorchester* was towed back to the vicinity of Long Point, where the cutter *Cape Horn* picked it up and brought it to MacMillan Wharf. Provincetown skin divers Red Murray and Martin Cordeiro, battling the severe conditions, worked on the propellers, but the *Dorchester* kept banging against the wharf, creating a dangerous situation. The *Dorchester* was forced to travel back and forth in the harbor for two days until work could resume.

The Mid-Cape Tornado of 1968

Marstons Mills was the site of a rare twentieth-century tornado, classified as an EF-1, on August 9, 1968. The *Cape Cod Standard-Times* reported that "baby" twisters were spotted, with witnesses calling it "a little frightening." No injuries were reported. Heavy rain, lightning strikes and high winds were reported in North Falmouth, Hyannis and Bourne, with significant damage reported in Marstons Mills, Cotuit, Mashpee, Waquoit and Sandwich.

1972: Tropical Storm Carrie

Moving off the East Coast of the United States on September 1, 1972, Tropical Storm Carrie began to lose strength before it was reinforced by "the approach of a new trough in the westerlies," according to a National Hurricane Center report. The storm made landfall in Eastport, Maine, on September 4, but not before unleashing torrential rainfall of six to nine inches on Cape Cod, along with wind gusts of forty-five to sixty knots, over Labor Day Weekend. According to the *Barnstable Patriot*, the Oyster Harbors' bridge gate blew off during the height of the storm, requiring emergency electrical repair to get the bridge working again.

The May Ice Storm of 1977

New Englanders thought winter was over as the calendar page turned to May in 1977, but Mother Nature had other ideas. The region was hit by a winter storm that dumped nearly two feet of snow in Worcester, Massachusetts, and nearly six inches along the Interstate 95 corridor. For Cape Codders, it was a nasty combination of snow, ice, rain, wind and high tides—and also a warning of what was to come at Eastham's Coast Guard Beach.

As a member of the Massachusetts Audubon Society's Wellfleet Bay Wildlife Sanctuary, Nan Turner Waldron, author of the book *Journey to Outermost House*, frequently stayed at Henry Beston's Outermost House on Coast Guard Beach for at least a couple of weeks every year between 1961 and 1977. As the storm approached, she noticed that the tides were abnormally high. "Something's wrong," she said to her husband, Ted. "There's a very high tide, and a big wind, and we are nowhere near high tide." Nan Turner Waldron wasn't the only one who noticed the abnormal elemental activity: "The day before, we noticed that there was not a bird, nothing."

Waldron would often say, "When you live that close to the sea, you better know what the sea is saying." She didn't stick around. "Fifteen years of times spent in that house had taught me that I should not wait to get out," she wrote in her book.

The next day, when the storm departed, Waldron returned and had to wade in water up to her shoulders to get back into the house. She noted that, since the house was built in 1925, it was the first time that sea water had reached the floor of the house.

"Ice, sleet, rain high winds, and twenty-foot waves tore open six gaps in the dunes," she wrote. Nine months later, Beston's literary landmark was lost in the February 1978 storm.

THE YARMOUTH TORNADO OF 1977

West Yarmouth was right in the path of a very brief EF-1 tornado, described as a "big black tunnel of air" by the *Cape Cod Standard-Times*, on August 21, 1977. The twister came ashore off Nantucket Sound at the Yarmouth Drive-In, blowing the theater's fourteen-foot sign across the street into the Parker's River Chowder House parking lot. Next in its path were the restaurant and the ART Barn Gallery, which lost its roof and walls. The twister then "spat out [the gallery's] paintings, sending them sailing down Parker's River." Doreen Miltenberger was in the gallery but remembered nothing after being found unconscious under the downed roof. One of the restaurant's customers was injured by flying glass.

HURRICANE GLORIA (1985)

Compared to the rest of Massachusetts, Cape Cod got off relatively easy with the arrival of Hurricane Gloria, which tracked over the Connecticut River Valley, far to the west. "If that storm had been just a little bit more to the east, Cape Cod wouldn't have fared so well," Scott Yuknis of Weather Service Corporation in Bedford, Massachusetts, told the *Cape Cod Times*.

"Hurricane Gloria may have turned out to be a lot of hot air," the *Cape Cod Oracle* said, noting that most of the damage came in the way of downed power lines, uprooted trees and a few boats running aground. Winds gusted up to one hundred miles per hour at the Chatham Coast Guard station, ninety-six miles per hour in Falmouth and seventy-five miles per hour in Wellfleet. Several buildings at the Lighthouse Inn in West Dennis were damaged, the inn reported, noting that the main building's dining room and several cottages needed new roofs. The *Cape Codder* reported someone took a Boston Whaler out of Priscilla Landing in Orleans toward Nauset Inlet to check a mooring. The boat flipped, but the operator was able to swim safely to shore.

NORTHEASTER OF DECEMBER 1990

Now that the storms of 1990 have unearthed, close to where I walked daily, the dwellings of a people much earlier than the Nausets, I ponder the idea of "ghostly remembrance" and spirit and connections.
—Nan Turner Waldron, Journey to Outermost House

The full moon has long been a factor in high tides, but when it's in the perigee position, as it was during the week after Thanksgiving 1990, and then you add a potent winter storm, the shoreline of Cape Cod was indeed at the mercy of the ocean.

Perigee is when the moon is at its closest position to the Earth. This helped to push the tides to slightly above twelve feet, the highest that Cape Cod saw in sixty years. On top of that, the storm surge and forty- to fifty-five-mile-per-hour winds added another three feet to high tide, according to the *Cape Cod Chronicle*.

The storm uncovered an ancient Native American campsite, according to the Cape Cod National Seashore. After the storm, archaeologist Geoff Carns was walking the beach when he noticed a stone fire pit. After some excavation, artifacts dating back 1,100 years were also found.

The excavation project began immediately due to the ongoing threat of erosion to the site, along with "the belief that the Carns site contained cultural components of great antiquity," the park's website stated. Over the next sixteen months, five episodes of fieldwork were conducted on portions of the Carns site.

The tides, which were three and a half feet above normal, also did extensive damage to Pucci's Restaurant, located on Provincetown's waterfront. The restaurant's enclosed deck was destroyed and the basement was flooded, according to the *Provincetown Advocate*. The wall facing the parking lot was close to collapsing, and parts of the walls facing the water were washed away.

The gale-force southwesterly wind added to the water's force, which also caused damage in the East End and Beach Point areas.

NORTHEASTER OF DECEMBER 1992

On December 12, 1992, shoppers at the Stop and Shop supermarket in Orleans were alerted with a public address announcement. Rather than the specials in the produce or deli department, they were told of something out of the ordinary, according to the *Cape Codder*: "Attention, shoppers. It is now high tide in the parking lot."

The supermarket is located near the Orleans/Eastham rotary, where an Outer Cape canal known as Jeremiah's Gutter once flowed. Tidal flooding is common in the north Orleans and South Eastham areas, but this storm was delivering tides that were well above the norm. By the time the system exited the area two days later, National Weather Service meteorologists were comparing it to previous storms such as the 1978 blizzard and the 1991 No-Name Storm. Hurricane-force wind gusts, very high tides and waves affected the coast from New Jersey to Massachusetts.

At Otis Air Force Base in Falmouth, a seventy-four-mile-per-hour gust was recorded. According to the National Weather Service Eastern Region Disaster Survey Report, "The Great Northeaster of December 1992," the Weather Service Meteorological Observatory at Chatham on Morris Island was cut off from the mainland by flooding from 2:00 p.m. on Saturday until Monday at 6:00 a.m. Sixty-mile-per-hour gusts were recorded there, but the anemometer was shadowed from the northeast by the radar dish. Meteorologists there conceded that the wind speeds were probably higher.

The dune at Ballston Beach in Truro, breached during the 1978 storm, was extended to a width of eighty-two feet. This once again turned North Truro and Provincetown into an island for three days, sending salt water into

Storm tides breach the dune at Truro's Ballston Beach into the Pamet River during the storm of December 1992. *Cape Cod National Seashore.*

the freshwater marsh and Pamet River, which flows westward to Cape Cod Bay. However, the raging storm surge wasn't the only attraction at Ballston Beach; a group of five pilot whales swam nearly two miles inland, going into the flooded Pamet River and becoming distressed near the Truro Post Office, the *Cape Cod Times* reported.

Stranding workers used a crane to lift two of the Pamet River whales onto a flatbed truck and took them to Herring Cove in Provincetown, where they were tagged and released. The other three whales died in the truck during the ten-mile drive to Herring Cove. Another eight pilot whales beached themselves in Provincetown Harbor, and five died. Another pair was beached near the Truro-Provincetown line. They were tagged and helped back into the water. Two whales were found in Brewster; one swam back to sea, and the other one died. Another whale beached in Eastham and perished. It was believed that the storm broke up a pod of whales offshore. The *Times* also reported a deep ocean bottlenose dolphin washed ashore near the Center for Coastal Studies in Provincetown.

In Chatham, the wind was "tossing around forty-foot fishing boats as if they were bath toys," in the words of the *Cape Cod Chronicle*. Claflin Landing was completely destroyed, but North Beach sustained only about one-third of the damage inflicted by the No-Name Storm fourteen months

Five pilot whales, disoriented by the storm of December 1992, swam nearly two miles up the Pamet River. *Cape Cod National Seashore.*

earlier. Route 28 in Harwich and South Orleans was closed due to flooding for two days in a row.

Sea salt was building up on utility wires, causing power outages and cable problems in Provincetown and Wellfleet, according to the *Cape Codder*. The roof was knocked off the Highland House in Truro. In Orleans, a traffic light was twisted to face the wrong direction.

Farther up the Cape, twenty feet of dune was reported lost in Sandwich, according to the National Weather Service Eastern Region Disaster Survey Report. Some residents were evacuated from areas of Barnstable, Falmouth and Wareham.

In Buzzards Bay, the 680-foot container ship *Chiara*, carrying 382,000 gallons of fuel, including corrosives, gases, liquids and flammables, scraped bottom by Stony Point Dike after exiting the Cape Cod Canal and was grounded for a day, the *Cape Cod Times* reported. The vessel was heading from Boston to New York.

When the ship took on water and began to list, the captain intentionally grounded it to prevent it from capsizing or sinking. Two empty fuel tanks torn open when the ship struck bottom were covered by mud after the vessel grounded near Nyes Neck in North Falmouth. The freighter was floated the following day. Even though the freighter that grounded in the Cape Cod

Canal was not a storm-related event, "its floatation was supported by tidal anomalies," the National Weather Service report said.

Off the coast of Chatham, the scalloper *Betty Ann* capsized and sank, with four fishermen being rescued from the twenty-foot swells by a Coast Guard helicopter.

HURRICANE EDOUARD (1996)

Cape Cod was enjoying its usual last days of summer when the National Weather Service issued a warning. Hurricane Edouard, which had been hugging the Eastern Seaboard for several days, was now predicted to hit the Cape on Labor Day.

So what happened? Massachusetts governor William Weld declared a state of emergency, followed by a traffic situation that led to the creation of the Commonwealth of Massachusetts Cape Cod Emergency Traffic Plan. According to the plan, "A six to eight-hour backup, stretching an estimated forty miles, occurred from the Sagamore Bridge to the Orleans Rotary along Route 6, due in large part to the challenges presented by the highway's rotaries and on-ramps."

During Sunday night, Edouard took an unexpected turn to the northeast, only brushing the Cape and totally sparing southeastern Massachusetts. Cape Cod didn't completely avoid hurricane-force winds; Commonwealth Electric lineman Tom Holmes of Hyannis, working a sixteen-hour shift restoring lines, referred to Edouard as "a northeaster without the snow," the *Cape Codder* said. Gusts reaching ninety miles per hour blew through Harwich, the *Cape Cod Times* reported. The *Register* said that the roof of the Hyannis Fire Department was partially blown off.

The *Register* also noted that Millway Beach in Barnstable looked like an ordinary summer day, with cars lining up, looking for a place to park. The main attractions were strong winds and high tides, as waves crashed over lifeguard stands and almost made it to the parking lot.

THE TWENTY-FIRST CENTURY

As a new millennium dawned across Cape Cod, the calendar may have changed, but the always-present threat of severe weather lashing the peninsula continued to loom large. While the rest of New England was hit by significant snowstorms early on, the Cape winters saw mostly less snowfall than the mainland.

Then came 2005, a year that featured two extremely unusual weather events. The following years, through 2023, would include some storybook storms as well.

This chapter includes observations from the author, who was either a full-time or part-time resident of Cape Cod from 2003 to 2023 and had the opportunity to experience several of these storms.

THE BLIZZARD OF JANUARY 2005

I lived in Siberia also, one year. Anything like this we never seen. NEVER.
—*Ashot Minasyan, as told to the* Cape Cod Times, *while stranded at Donut Works in Hyannis, January 25, 2005*

Wellfleet police sergeant Bob Hussey, a resident of the Outer Cape since 1974, didn't mince words when asked by the *Cape Cod Times* about the monster snowstorm of January 24, 2005. "This is the most snow I've ever seen on the Cape," he said.

The Blizzard of January 2005 dumped nearly three feet of snow across some areas of Cape Cod, creating a tough shoveling situation outside the Eastham Four Points Sheraton. *Author's collection.*

Nearly three feet of snow fell in a twenty-four-hour period, piling snowdrifts up to ten to fifteen feet high. Winds gusted to eighty-four miles per hour, with seas producing waves up to twenty-seven feet. Local emergency response workers and snowplow drivers were overwhelmed. For the first time in its history, the *Cape Cod Times* was unable to deliver that day's editions the following morning. It would be several days before many secondary roads were plowed. In 2019, James Freeman, writing for *Cape Cod Life Magazine*, quoted the journal of longtime meteorologist Tim Kelley, a Cape native: "Blizzard '05 worst on Cape in my life." Cape resident Charles Orloff, executive director of the Blue Hill Weather Observatory in Milton, Massachusetts, told the *Times* that he had "never seen snow this deep and drifts this high on the Cape."

As the storm was hitting on January 24, Jon March of Connecticut decided to brave the storm and drive to his cottage in Eastham. The next day, March took a trip with the author around the Outer Cape. The author's recollection of March's adventure follows:

On his way to the Cape, March used his four-wheel drive "Outermost Van" and wire cable to pull a plow that was stuck in the snow in Wareham.

Upon arrival to his cottage on the Outer Cape, he was greeted by a seven-foot wall of snow. After digging that out for forty-five minutes, he barreled through and found himself stuck, leading to another half-hour or so of digging. That concluded at about 3:30 a.m.

The following day, the waves at Coast Guard Beach in Eastham were monstrous, and that was down a notch from the day before, when the storm was still raging. The ocean had completely washed over the barrier beach, as only slushy ice covered the sand and grass of the dunes. Large logs and tree trunks, caked in thick ice, were strewn everywhere.

While the snow totals far exceeded the Blizzard of '78 on the Cape, coastal damage was not nearly as severe. "Tides were not as high [as 1978] and there was minimal coastal flooding," the *Times* reported.

The "Sting Jet Storm" of 2005

On Friday, December 9, 2005, the New England region was hit by what seemed to be a typical northeaster. Across the Boston area, close to a foot of snow fell, while on Cape Cod, frozen precipitation amounts were minimal. By early afternoon, the sun had begun to emerge from behind the clouds. Then, the weather took an unusual turn.

The skies darkened, and wind gusts reached close to one hundred miles per hour in some spots. According to the *Cape Cod Times*, trees were laying across roads, crushing cars, while many other roads became impassable because of downed wires. Power went out for fifty thousand homes.

So what happened? David R. Vallee of the Boston-area National Weather Service office in Taunton would later author a report called "The Coastal Bomb of December 9th, 2005: So What Was That Thing That Hit Us?" The Weather Service would also refer to it as a "Sting Jet Storm." The storm, which passed through New England, intensified at an abnormally fast pace as it approached Cape Cod. Glenn Field, the warning coordination meteorologist of the Boston National Weather Service office, provided the details in a 2023 interview:

The storm was at 1010 millibars, but three hours later it's 992 millibars. It drops 13 millibars in three hours. It continued on four more millibars two hours after that. A normal bombogenesis is 24 millibars in 24 hours. The

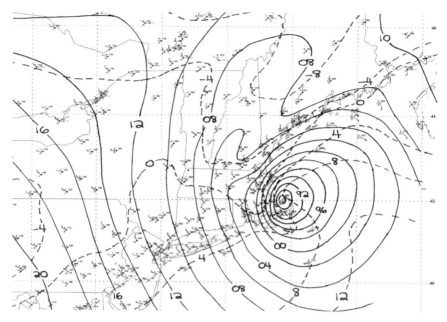

A weather map shows the convection around Cape Cod Bay during the "Sting Jet" storm of December 2005. *NOAA.*

rate of deepening was four times more than a bombogenesis. It was moving unbelievably fast.

According to Vallee's report, two storms were involved: the primary low-pressure area in the Ohio Valley and a secondary low-pressure area moving up the coast from the Carolinas. The evolution then continued this way, Vallee noted:

- *Tremendous synoptic scale support;*
- *Upper level disturbance and associated Tropopause Fold excites rapid intensification as the secondary low approaches southeast New England;*
- *Perfect conditions for Mesoscale Snow Band formation in the comma head;*
- *Slantwise convection in some way emulated downburst mechanics seen in upright convection;*
- *Result: "The Sting at the end of the Tail."*

Cape Cod was about to get stung.

High wind gust reports from the National Weather Service included 101 miles per hour in Wellfleet, 100 in Orleans, 96 in Eastham, 89 in Brewster,

76 in Yarmouth Port and 75 in Chatham. The *Cape Cod Times* reported that fishing docks that were stacked in Bourne's Monument Beach Marina parking lot for the winter were swept out of the lot by a tidal surge onto Emmons Road.

Amy Corcoran of West Brewster was driving her car on Route 6A, near the Cape Cod Sea Camps in Brewster, when a tree branch hit her car. Corcoran, seven months pregnant, also had her four-year-old daughter in the vehicle. According to the *Cape Codder*, Corcoran pulled into the Sea Camps driveway, where camp staff invited her into the facility. School buses filled with students also took over in the driveway. All of them were provided food and blankets by the camp staff, along with an offer to stay the night, if needed. All of them stayed until about 7:00 p.m. There was a similar scene at Laurino's Pizza in Brewster, where a busload of students was treated to pizza while waiting out the storm. The *Cape Codder* also told the story of Renita and Dennis O'Connell, who were shopping at Stop and Shop in Orleans when the storm hit. When the store staff realized the customers were going to be stranded, they were invited up to the conference room, with a backup generator, and were treated to a buffet feast.

Meanwhile, the storm was also making life miserable for sea mammals in Cape Cod Bay. Twenty-three dolphins and fifteen pilot whales were beached, the *Cape Codder* reported. Kristen Patchett of the Cape Cod Stranding Network speculated that it was a combination of the high winds, tides, shallows and foraging. These mammals often travel in groups, she said, and may have been confused by the storm conditions.

December is also the middle of sea turtle stranding season along Cape Cod bay beaches, but only two of the reptiles were beached in the storm. The surviving turtle was a sixty-pound loggerhead turtle in Wellfleet.

In the area of woods along Nauset Road and Doane Road in Eastham, which leads to the Cape Cod National Seashore's Coast Guard Beach, several trees were leveled by the hurricane-force winds. As of 2023, these dead trees still litter the woods, particularly east of Doane Rock, as a reminder of the "Sting Jet Storm" of 2005.

THE PATRIOTS DAY STORM OF 2007

In addition to commemorating the early battles of the Revolutionary War, Patriots Day is also known as Boston Marathon Day in Massachusetts.

On Cape Cod, it's also remembered for a storm that tore a new inlet in Chatham Bar.

According to the *Cape Cod Chronicle*, the new breach was north of the break created by the January 1987 storm, off Allen Point in North Chatham, and transformed North Beach into an island. The new break caused tremendous currents in Pleasant Bay, rapidly accelerating the erosion process and the demise of the Chatham beach camp community. During the storm, the Scott family's camp was swept away.

According to the National Weather Service, the Cape saw east to northeast winds gusting from fifty to sixty miles per hour, with East Falmouth reaching sixty-seven miles per hour.

TROPICAL STORM IRENE (2011)

Copious amounts of rain fell across New England as Tropical Storm Irene pushed its way through Western Massachusetts on August 26 and 27, 2011, but most areas of Cape Cod received less than an inch of rain. Irene made landfall at Coney Island in New York, where it quickly lost its hurricane status before crossing into Connecticut and Massachusetts. Highest wind gusts reached about sixty miles per hour on the Cape.

Two men brave the gale-force winds from Tropical Storm Irene at Glendon Street Beach in Dennis Port in August 2011. *Author's collection.*

A large cabin cruiser and powerboat ran aground on the beach in Onset, thanks to the high winds, the *Cape Cod Times* reported. In Hyannis, a sailboat grounded near the Hyannis Yacht Club after breaking free from its mooring. Along Route 6A in Barnstable, a 250-year-old beech tree fell on the historic Daniel Davis house, which had renovation work completed just two days earlier.

Super Storm Sandy (2012)

Hurricane Sandy, also referred to as "Super Storm Sandy," is perhaps best known for the disaster inflicted on New York and New Jersey during the final week of October 2012. However, the storm affected the entire East Coast from Florida to Maine, providing a "sideswipe of New England," according to meteorologist Glenn Field of the National Weather Service's Boston-area office in Norton, Massachusetts.

At Sandy Neck in Barnstable, the storm surge reached the dune line, but the bayside beach "dodged a bullet on that one," park manager Nina Coleman told the *Cape Cod Times*. That was pretty much the consensus for the entire Cape, Field said in a 2023 interview: "Sandy had forty-five-foot waves offshore, breaking at twenty-five feet onshore. There was a five-foot storm surge, but it moved a tremendous amount of sand."

The National Weather Service reported a severe thunderstorm embedded in an outer band associated with Sandy produced wind gusts to ninety miles per hour and concentrated damage in Wareham, along with an eighty-three-mile-per-hour gust at a buoy located off Cuttyhunk Island and eighty-one miles per hour in Wellfleet. The *Times* noted wind speeds of seventy-nine miles per hour at Marstons Mills and Barnstable, seventy-two at East Falmouth, sixty-two at Falmouth and sixty-one at Hyannis.

Other areas took a beating during the day, including a small building on the Hyannisport Yacht Club dock that was destroyed in the powerful surf. Nauset Beach in Orleans was pounded by ten- to twelve-foot waves, but the main stretch of public beach was largely spared significant erosion.

THE NORTHEASTER OF FEBRUARY 2013

Given the name "Nemo" by the Weather Channel, this storm began a string of northeasters that carried on until mid-March. By the time it was all said and done by spring's arrival, twenty feet of shoreline was sliced off the Cape's perimeter, the *Cape Cod Times* reported. Thanks to these gales, many seaside houses had to be demolished, and several barrier beaches were breached.

Beginning on February 8, the first storm delivered seventeen inches of snow and astronomically high tides, with coastal areas being hammered by 20- to 25-foot waves. Wind gusts topped out at eighty-four miles per hour on Cuttyhunk Island, eighty-three in Falmouth and seventy-seven in Hyannis. Eighty-mile-per-hour winds and tides 4 feet above normal punched a hole through Chatham's South Beach, the *Cape Cod Chronicle* noted. The breaks were said to be 850 feet wide and 750 feet wide. North Beach's dunes were flattened, and the beach camp owned by Alice Adams was knocked on its side.

Other beaches breached included Ballston Beach in Truro and Town Neck in Sandwich, where the Sandwich Boardwalk sustained severe damage. In Dennis, nearly fifteen to twenty feet of shoreline was washed away from bayside beaches, and portions of Dr. Bottero Road were sliced up by the surf, the *Register* reported.

THE DEEP FREEZE STORMS OF 2015

In December 2014, the Town of Barnstable added four thousand cubic yards of sand to the dunes of Sandy Neck Beach, at a cost of $90,000, per the *Register*. By the end of January, it was gone in one shot.

After an abnormally cold November, December and most of January were relatively tame for Cape Cod winter standards. Then came the storm of January 25, which was christened "Juno" by the Weather Channel. This storm began a brutal run of storms and severe Arctic chill that didn't end until April. Nearly two feet of snow fell, and high tides pushed by wind gusts of fifty-five to seventy-five miles per hour left the peninsula paralyzed.

Sandy Neck was just one of the coastal locations that was clobbered. Among the damage reported by WCAI-FM in Woods Hole were several homes on Town Neck Beach in Sandwich, dunes at Sesuit Beach in Dennis and Ballston Beach in Truro and the stairway at Nauset Light Beach in

Eastham. Coastal flooding closed Route 28 in East Harwich and Chatham Port, while Chatham's east-facing beaches suffered extensive erosion, the *Cape Cod Chronicle* reported. Over-washes were the worst since the 2007 storm, the paper added.

The boathouse at the end of Cotchpinicut Road was swept away, with only the pilings remaining. "The roof's in the marsh," Chatham harbormaster Stuart Smith told the *Chronicle*. Somehow, the last two camps on North Beach Island survived.

If that storm wasn't enough, another storm followed on February 9. This storm featured hurricane-force wind gusts in twelve locations, topped by eighty-three-mile-per-hour winds at Cuttyhunk Island. Sandy Neck Beach, Millway Beach and Blish Point in Barnstable all sustained significant damage, while a stairway leading to Sandy Neck Beach was destroyed, the *Barnstable Patriot* reported.

Thirty inches of snow fell on some parts of the Cape, with drifts piling ten to twelve feet. John Norman spent twenty-four hours plowing for a private contractor. "I saw things I had never seen in 20 years of moving snow," he told the *Patriot*. "There were snowdrifts so large they overwhelmed six-wheeled dump trucks."

The Tasha shack of Provincetown, formerly owned by the Bohemian poet Harry Kemp, saw its walls blown out by the severe storms in the winter of 2015. *Author's collection.*

Chapin Beach in Dennis lost twenty feet of beach in some areas, the *Register* reported. An area that had washed over in a previous storm halfway down the beach was widened, and the entrance ramp was damaged beyond repair. Dr. Bottero Road, the road that leads up to Chapin Beach, also washed out.

In the dunes of Provincetown, the author, in May 2015, observed significant storm damage done to the tiny Tasha dune shack. The structure lost its windows and an entire wall. The shack was bequeathed to the Tasha family by the poet Harry Kemp following his death in 1960.

THE HIGH TIDE STORMS OF 2018

The winter of 2018 began in January with a storm that featured hurricane-force winds and a fifteen-foot storm tide. This resulted in coastal flooding around the Cape, particularly Chatham.

The situation repeated itself with a sequence of northeasters in March that arrived along with abnormally high tides, changing the coast forever. At Nauset Beach in Orleans, these two storms swallowed up to sixty feet of shoreline, Orleans natural resources manager Nathan Sears told the *Cape Cod Times.*

Of all the shoreline devastation left in the winter of 2018's wake, the loss of Liam's (formerly Philbrick's) Snack Shack on Nauset Beach may be the most memorable. "The tide cycle from Friday night to noon on Saturday took almost every bit of the beach," Liam's owner John Ohman told the *Cape Cod Times.* "In thirteen hours, it transformed the entire beach." Liam's, famous for its onion rings, hung on the edge of the sand for a couple of weeks before it was demolished. According to the *Times*, there was 250 feet of beach between the shack and sea in 1954. Google Earth showed there was 160 feet to the beach in 2008, 109 in 2014 and just 80 in 2017, the *Times* noted.

Orleans police lieutenant Kevin Higgins, a lifelong Orleans resident, told the *Cape Cod Chronicle* he had never seen Nauset Beach breach by the parking lot, into the lower RV lot and into the Pochet River. Water surged through the marsh into Pleasant Bay, wiping out dunes that were twenty to thirty feet high.

During the snack shack's final days, many in town drove to the beach for a final look. Cape Cod photographer Danya Mahota noted in a Facebook post: "Nauset was sad today…people huddled, hugging, crying."

The severe storms of March 2018 were the death blow for Liam's Snack Shack (formerly Philbrick's) at Nauset Beach in Orleans. *Author's collection.*

The *Provincetown Independent* recalled in 2022 the 2018 storm's impact on Provincetown, noting the storm surge "turned Gosnold Street into a river of seawater and a stretch of Bradford Street near town hall into a four-foot-deep lake."

At Nauset Light Beach in North Eastham, a longtime vacation house across from the lighthouse had to be demolished, as the structure was left nearly hanging off the bluff. To the south of the parking lot, the new path to the beach, which replaced the several sets of staircases lost to previous storms, immediately felt nature's impact, according to the author's observations:

> *A rogue wave that powered its way over the dune either knocked over or soaked several people observing the stormy conditions at the entrance to the beach. Two people fell into the path of the incoming water. Another large crashing wave sent many of the onlookers dashing up the path for safety.*

Barry Desilets, owner of the Colors of Chatham Gallery in Chatham, backed away from the beach as the waves approached. However, when some of the onlookers remained in the flooded area, he was left shaking his head.

"This one guy was caught in that, with water up to here," Desilets recalled in October 2023, holding his hand level with his chest. "He yelled out, 'God, give me another one!' I couldn't believe it."

NORTHEASTER/TROPICAL STORM WANDA (2021)

Cape Cod was walloped by a northeaster on October 27, 2021, that later grew into Tropical Storm Wanda in the open Atlantic Ocean. The storm lashed the Cape with eighty-mile-per-hour wind gusts, taking down trees and power lines from the Cape Cod Canal to Provincetown. Several towns were either completely or nearly without power. Eversource reported 152,000 outages Cape-wide, with a sole source circuit outage on the Outer Cape resulting in whole-town outages for Truro and Provincetown.

According to the National Hurricane Center, the storm "became a subtropical cyclone a few days after moving away from the United States and underwent tropical transition while it meandered over the open waters of the North Atlantic Ocean."

In Barnstable, a woman became trapped in her car when a tree fell on it, but she was uninjured, according to WHDH-TV. Several trees dating back to the 1800s were leveled. The *Provincetown Independent* reported that a two-hundred-year-old Siberian elm at Truro Vineyards was taken down. Wellfleet, which was hit by eighty-three-mile-per-hour wind gusts, lost several trees that dated back to the 1800s. Highland Light in Truro, which was undergoing renovations at the time of the storm, saw the scaffolding that was wrapped around the tower peeled off by the high winds.

THE PROVINCETOWN FLOOD OF 2022

Pucci's Restaurant in Provincetown took on a storm surge in 1990. Pucci's would later reemerge as Fanizzi's Restaurant by the Sea, but similar devastation awaited the bayside location just before Christmas 2022. Fanizzi's and the East End Market on Bradford Street were among those hardest hit by the storm of December 23, 2022.

The storm's south winds brought above-average temperatures but also high waves that smashed into harbor-side buildings. Fanizzi's was flooded with three feet of water, while seawater flowed in as far as Bradford Street. Water began trickling into the East End Market, and within thirty seconds, there was a foot of water, the *Provincetown Independent* said.

Twenty-First-Century Tornadoes

The second decade of the twenty-first century saw an increase in tornado activity on Cape Cod, with five twisters rolling through the region between 2018 and 2023.

Tornado warnings were posted for the Cape on the night of July 22, 2019, but the twisters never materialized. At midday on July 23, new warnings were issued, and EF-1 tornadoes touched down in three locations between West Yarmouth and East Harwich. One of the highlights of local, regional and national newscasts was the roof being ripped from the Cape Sands Inn on Route 28 in West Yarmouth.

According to the National Weather Service's Damage Survey Report from July 23, a super cell thunderstorm was producing waterspouts over Vineyard Sound and Nantucket Sound, with one of them moving ashore just west of Kalmus Beach in Hyannis. The twister lifted after going through West Yarmouth but returned to ground level again in South Yarmouth, causing significant damage to the area just southeast of Dennis-Yarmouth High School. Areas along Hazelmoor Road from Violet Glen Road to Vine Brook Road were particularly hard hit. Dozens of trees were uprooted, and a few were snapped off.

In South Yarmouth, Cheryl Falconer was sitting in her car, about three or four miles from her home, at Smugglers' Beach just before noon, when her phone rang. It was her daughter calling, informing her of the tornado warning. Falconer recalled in a 2023 correspondence how the weather conditions worsened rapidly:

> *The light rain turned to heavy rain, blowing sand and rain almost horizontal. Now I'm too far to make it to my house, and my friend lived about ¾ mile away, so I head to her house. I'm petrified, but calm. Now, which road do I take to get there? The trees are bending, some branches have fallen, which I drove around. I get to her house. The minute I get out of the car I'm socked. I run to the door, locked, and no answer. I run around back and got in. When it was over I drove home. I guess I picked the right road to travel, as the other two had trees down in the road.*

The staff at the Lighthouse Inn in West Dennis also had closer encounters with the tornadoes than they would have liked. In the Lighthouse Inn's historical dateline, the owners recalled:

Greg Stone and others saw the tornado as it came across the water in front of the inn. Deb Stone Haines was on her bike in South Yarmouth, jumped into a hedge, and put her bike over her head to shield herself from the wind. When she came out of the hedge, massive trees had fallen on both ends of the road she was on. It took her approximately one hour to get back to the inn two miles away, carrying her bike over downed trees and power lines.

The inn lost power for three days and sustained significant tree damage on the road and around the building. According to the inn's history account, "Furniture blew through Room 11's window, the bench near the shuffleboard court blew down to the jetty on the east side of the property, lounge chairs ended up in the ocean, and the fire pit glass enclosure was lost."

Around Bass River, the tornado lifted, but severe straight-line wind damage occurred from West Dennis to West Harwich. Numerous trees were uprooted, consistent with ninety-mile-per-hour gusts.

The National Weather Service reported that the twister took shape again near Harwich Center, just east of Harwich Elementary School and south of Parallel Street. The 250-foot tornado, packing winds of 110 miles per hour, then moved 2.77 miles northeastward along Route 39 before lifting in East Harwich near Queen Anne Road. Severe straight-line wind damage continued into Chatham. The *Cape Cod Chronicle* told the story of a school bus, carrying eight children, pulled into an Agway store in Chatham after Nicole Hedmark, the summer camp program leader, received a tornado warning on her phone. The group stayed in the store's interior until the storm passed.

The 2019 tornadoes were sandwiched by two other storms. An EF-0 twister came ashore in Woods Hole in October 2018, when four large wooden chairs were hurled about five hundred feet at the Woods Hole Golf Club, according to the *Cape Cod Times*. On September 1, 2021, a minor tornado, powered by the remnants of Hurricane Ida, hit the bayside area near Corporation Beach in Dennis, with the seventy-five-mile-per-hour storm damaging a small area concentrated near the intersection of East Bay View Road and Wampanoag Trail.

Another EF-0 tornado plowed through Marstons Mills just before noon on August 8, 2023. According to the National Weather Service Damage

Survey Report, the storm, 650 yards wide, lasted four minutes and traveled just over a mile, beginning at Evergreen Drive and following a northeasterly track before lifting at Joe Thompson Road. The report listed the damage as follows:

> *The primary damage indicators were an uprooted hardwood tree and a downed electrical pole, supplemented by strewn debris inclusive of smaller trees, fence posts, and branches. The damage was most concentrated near the center of the track at the intersection of Race Lane and Osterville–West Barnstable Road. Witnesses described a chaotic event, observing airborne fence posts and branches.*

EPILOGUE

Sometimes the sea becomes furiously angry. At the Farm House, we awaken, to find the wind blowing straight out of the northeast and driving rain before it. On such a day, anyone with any sense would "hole in" and spend the day on household tasks, or read, or play cribbage.
Instead of doing this, however, we are likely for some strange reason to take the car and drive to the Coast Guard Station.
—*Wyman Richardson,* The House on Nauset Marsh

When it comes to being alert of incoming storms, there may not be anyone who pays more attention to the weather forecasts than Cape Codders. When the storms hit, Cape Codders are at the beaches, viewing the elements with awe. When the high winds and heavy snow and rain pass, nobody continues to tell the stories more than Cape Codders.

All over the Cape, the reminders are there. Along the shores of Town Cove in Eastham, only footsteps away from the Orleans border, is the Collins Cove cottage colony. Built in the 1920s by longtime Life-Saving Service and Coast Guard surfman Lewis Collins and his son, Bernard, the colony also has what's referred to as a "shucking house," where Kenelm Collins began a long tradition of recording the impact of northeasters. According to the *Cape Codder*, "He marks the level storms have reached in his garage the way some measure the growth of children. The '78 storm is marked about shin high. The big storm of '87 is waist high. The marks of '91 need no ink; they cover the garage."

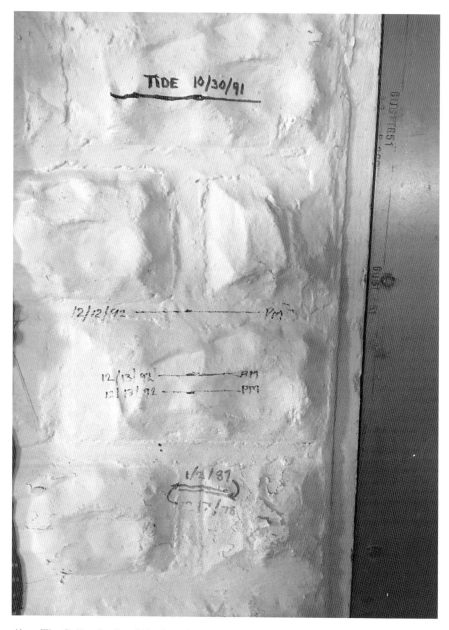

Above: The Collins family of Eastham has a long tradition of recording the measurements of storm tides inside their "shucking house" along Collins Cove. *Author's collection.*

Opposite: The storm of 1978 is the storm of record for the Outer Cape, according to former Eastham natural resources officer Henry Lind. *Cape Cod National Seashore.*

There's a similar fascination on the Mid-Cape. A gauge for hurricanes lurks inside the storage shed at Crosby's Landing in Osterville. According to the *Cape Cod Times* in 1989, David Webber pointed out the series of lines on the wall that show the levels of water left by those storms. Donna Edson, who, along with her husband, barely escaped from North Beach in Chatham during the No-Name Storm, told the *Register* that she gives that event the nod over the storms of 1978 and 1987.

While these measurements were certainly as close to the experience as one can get, they don't fall into the category of "official." David Aubrey, director of the Coastal Research Center at the Woods Hole Oceanographic Institution, told the *Cape Cod Times* that the No-Name Storm of 1991 fell into the classification of "one-hundred-year storm," a severity index typically used by engineers and regulators. The term is used to describe a storm that has a one-in-one-hundred chance of occurring each year. As Aubrey told the *Cape Cod Times*: "[Hurricane] Bob was the storm of record for Falmouth, whereas, for Chatham the storm would be this one…[which] was somehow complicated by not only by a high-pressure center to the northwest, but also Hurricane Grace."

During a 2008 interview, Henry Lind, Eastham's longtime natural resources officer, sorted it out this way:

[The '78 storm] *definitely remains the storm of record for this area, the Lower Cape. The storm of record is considered a 100-year effort, and that 100-year storm is a computer model, based on potential wind speed, precipitation, sea level, wave action. It's based on best-guessed estimates of the wind blowing and the speed, and the fetch over which it is blowing. In 1990 and '91, we had two back-to-back, just from the still water elevation, that were pretty close to that. But from all the other perspectives, of the duration of the storm, damage done by erosion, flooding, etc., the '78 storm is the storm of record.*

In 1992, Tom Leach, Harwich's longtime harbormaster, offered a warning of dire consequences, reported by the *Cape Codder*, shortly after the one-two punch of the 1991 storms: "The storms of 1991 serve as a graphic reminder that, despite our abilities to move mountains, forest, and rivers, we as a species are still very much a part of an environment that can deliver forces far exceeding most of our puny efforts."

Following Hurricane Bob's quick but powerful hit on the Cape in August 1991, the *Cape Codder* contacted Jane Simard, director of the Orleans Senior Center, to see how the local elderly people were faring. They were just fine, she told the paper: "The seniors didn't have any problems. They all know what to do. It's young people like us who had to figure things out. We think we live in such a sophisticated world. But nature humbles us."

BIBLIOGRAPHY

Books

And Bob Was His Name: Hurricane Bob, a Diary of Destruction, August 19, 1991. Sun City West, AZ: C.F. Boone Publishing Company, 1991.

Beston, Henry. *The Outermost House.* New York: Doubleday, 1928.

Cann, Donald J., and John Galluzzo. *Images of America: Camp Edwards and Otis Air Force Base.* Charleston, SC: Arcadia Publishing, 2010.

Higgins, Frances L. *Drifting Memories: The Nauset Beach Camps on Cape Cod.* Orleans, MA: Lower Cape Publishing, 1996.

Reid, Nancy Thacher. *Dennis, Cape Cod: From Firstcomers to Newcomers, 1639–1993.* Dennis, MA: Dennis Historical Society, 1996.

Richardson, Wyman, and Henry B. Kane. *The House on Nauset Marsh.* Woodstock, VT: Countryman Press, 2005.

Vorse, Mary Heaton. *Time and the Town: A Provincetown Chronicle.* New Brunswick, NJ: Rutgers University Press, 1996 (originally 1942).

Waldron, Nan Turner. *Journey to Outermost House.* Bethlehem, CT: Butterfly and Wheel Publishing, 1991.

Whatley, Michael E. *Marconi Wireless on Cape Cod: South Wellfleet, MA, 1901–1917.* Washington, D.C. National Park Service, 1988.

Periodicals

Barnstable Patriot, Hyannis, MA: August 28, 1924; January 8, 1931; September 24, 1936; September 21, 1944; September 28, 1944; September 14, 1950; September 2, 1954; September 16, 1954; September 15, 1960; June 20, 2003.

Boston Globe, September 25, 1944; September 26, 1944; January 3, 1987; August 20, 1991; August 21, 1991; August 22, 1991; November 10, 1991; June 4, 2007.

Boston Herald, August 27, 1991.

Bourne Courier, Bourne, MA: June 5, 1991; August 20, 1991.

Cape Cod Chronicle, Chatham, MA: September 29, 1938; February 9, 1978; February 16, 1978; December 6, 1990; December 17, 1992; January 4, 2017.

Cape Codder, Orleans, MA: September 26, 1944; September 14, 1950; September 2, 1954; January 26, 1961; May 12, 1977; February 10, 1978; January 2, 1979; September 28, 1985; January 6, 1987; February 10, 1987; December 7, 1990; November 1, 1991; January 24, 1992; September 6, 1996; February 15, 2002; December 9, 2005.

Cape Cod Life, Hyannis, MA: August/September 1987; January 1992.

Cape Cod News, February 1, 1933.

Cape Cod Oracle, Harwich, MA: October 10, 1985.

Cape Cod Standard-Times, Hyannis, MA: September 15, 1944; September 13, 1960; August 21, 1977.

Cape Cod Times, Hyannis, MA: September 28, 1985; January 3, 1987; August 31, 1989; August 22, 1991; October 31, 1991; November 1, 1991; November 3, 1991; December 12, 1992; December 13, 1992; December 14, 1992; March 15, 1993; September 3, 1996; February 7, 1998; October 31, 2001; January 25, 2005; December 10, 2005; August 30, 2014; January 5, 2018.

Central Cape Press, Harwich, MA: September 14, 1950; September 2, 1954.

Dennis-Yarmouth Register, Yarmouth, MA: September 16, 1960.

Falmouth Enterprise, Falmouth, MA: August 30, 1924; September 23, 1938; September 30, 1938; September 22, 1944; September 3, 1954; September 13, 1960; August 10, 1976; August 23, 1991.

Harwich Independent, Harwich, MA: September 29, 1938; October 6, 1938; September 21, 1944.

Hyannis Patriot, Hyannis, MA: September 22, 1938.

Martha's Vineyard Magazine, Martha's Vineyard, MA: September–October 2003.

Naval History Magazine, U.S. Naval Institute: February 2000.

New Bedford Standard-Times, New Bedford, MA: October 1, 1938.

New York Times, August 13, 1917; August 27, 1924.

Provincetown Advocate, Provincetown, MA: January 8, 1931; September 29, 1938; September 21, 1944; September 2, 1954; January 26, 1961; January 27, 1966; December 6, 1990; August 22, 1991; November 7, 1991.

Provincetown Independent, Provincetown, MA: December 29, 2022.

The Register, Yarmouth, MA: September 29, 1983; January 8, 1987; December 6, 1990; August 29, 1991; November 7, 1991; September 5, 1996.

Taunton Daily Gazette. "The Complete Historical Record of New England's Stricken Area: September 21, 1938." September 1938.

Village Advertiser, Osterville, MA: September 18, 1983.

Village Broadsider, Sandwich, MA: January 7, 1987.

Yarmouth Register, Yarmouth, MA: November 30, 1901; June 25, 1904; August 18, 1917; August 27, 1924; September 30, 1938; September 22, 1944; September 29, 1944; October 6, 1944; September 3, 1954; September 17, 1954.

Personal Interviews by the Author

Beyle, Noel. Eastham, MA, January 2008.
Clarke, Jack. Boston, January 2008.
Desilets, Barry. Chatham, MA, October 2023.
Dill, Tommy. Eastham, MA, June 2016.
DuPertuis, Lydia (Moore). Northbridge, MA, July 2018.
Ersoy, Linda. Provincetown, MA, May 2023.
Field, Glenn. Norton, MA, June 2023.
Finch, Robert. Wellfleet, MA, April 2014.
Giese, Graham. Franklin, MA, June 2023.
Lind, Henry. Eastham, MA, January 2008.
Seay, Bob. Eastham, MA, January 2008.

Reports and Articles

Board of Underwater Archaeological Resources. *Vineyard* lightship.
Commonwealth of Massachusetts. "The Worst Hurricanes of the 20th Century."
www.mass.gov/service-details/the-worst-massachusetts-hurricanes-of-the-
20th-century.
Federal Writers' Project of the Works Progress Administration in the New
England States. "New England Hurricane: A Factual Pictorial Record."
Boston: Hale, Cushman, & Flint, 1938.
Lighthouse Inn. "History Time Line for Bass River Light and Lighthouse
Inn, 1854–2018." West Dennis, MA.
National Park Service. "Coastal Geomorphology Storms of Record: The
Perfect Storm (1991)." www.nps.gov/articles/the-perfect-storm-1991.
htm.
National Weather Service. "The Blizzard of '78 Revisited." Taunton, MA.
———. "Hurricane Threat—New England Perspective/New England?—
Just a Matter of Time." Norton, MA.
———. "July 22 and 23, 2019: Two Severe Weather Events Impact Cape
Cod but with Vastly Different Outcomes." Norton, MA.
———. "The 'Patriot's Day' Coastal Storm of April 15–17, 2007." Taunton,
MA.
NOAA. "Natural Disaster Survey Report: The Halloween Nor'easter."
1992.
NOAA Miami Regional Library. "Monthly Weather Review—Annual
Summaries of North Atlantic Storms, 1872–2011: October 28 to
November 1, 1991." National Hurricane Center, Miami, FL, June 1992.
Simpson, R.H., and Paul J. Hebert. "Atlantic Hurricane Season of 1972."
National Hurricane Center, National Weather Service, NOAA, Miami,
FL. www.nhc.noaa.gov/data/mwreview/1972.pdf.
Unidentified newspaper article in scrapbook of Eva Leslie Grew, Nickerson
Archives, Cape Cod Community College, West Barnstable, MA.
Vallee, David. "The Coastal Bomb of December 9th, 2005: So What Was
That Thing That Hit Us?" National Weather Service, Taunton, MA,
January 2006.
Woods Hole Sea Grant Program. "Hurricane Vs. Nor'easter." Cape
Cod Cooperative Extension, Woods Hole, MA. Hurricane_Vs._
Noreaster_6-19_FINAL_125504.pdf.

Newsletters

The Acorn. Sandwich Historical Society, Sandwich, MA, 1973 (reprinted in the *Cape Cod Independent*, January 1978).
The Crow's Nest. Mattapoisett Museum, Mattapoisett, MA, May 25, 2021
The Fog Horn. U.S. Coast Guard Lightship Sailors Association, 2011.

Websites

Board of Underwater Archaeological Resources, Commonwealth of Massachusetts. "Vineyard Sound Lightship." www.mass.gov/service-details/vineyard-sound-lightship.
The Moors Association, Falmouth, MA. www.themoors1925.org.
National Park Service. "Cape Cod National Seashore." nps.gov/caco.

Author's Correspondence

Champlin, Mildred. October 2023.
Chapman, Steve. September 2023.
Clarke, Jack. October 2023.
Falconer, Cheryl. August 2023.
Nickerson, Gail. September 2023.

Exhibits

Nickerson Beach Camp. Atwood House Museum, Chatham Historical Society, Chatham, MA.

Television Programs

Books and the World. Cape Cod Writers Center, Barnstable, MA, 1991.

Radio Reports

WCAI-FM. Woods Hole, MA, February 2015.

Social Media Posts

Danya Mahota. Facebook, March 2018.
National Weather Service. Facebook, "On This Day in Weather History, August 17, 2023 (1917 gale)."
———. Facebook, "On This Day in Weather History, Sept. 21–22, 1961."

INDEX

ABOUT THE AUTHOR

Since the start of the millennium, Don Wilding has been telling stories of Cape Cod Outer Beach history. An award-winning writer and editor for Massachusetts newspapers for thirty-six years, Don is the author of four other books on Cape Cod history, including *Shipwrecks of Cape Cod: Stories of Tragedy and Triumph* and *Cape Cod and the Portland Gale of 1898*. He has worked as a tour guide and leads history walks for the Harwich Conservation Trust at Cape Cod National Seashore. Don and his wife, Nita, live in Franklin, Massachusetts, and in Dennis on Cape Cod.

Visit us at
www.historypress.com
....